BRITISH GEOLOGICAL SURVEY

S J MATHERS
A HORTON
C R BRISTOW

Geology of the country around Diss

Memoir for 1:50 000 geological sheet 175
(England and Wales)

CONTRIBUTORS

D K Graham
Hydrogeology

T E Lawson
R A Monkhouse
R J Wyatt
J A Zalasiewicz

LONDON: HMSO   1993

First published 1993

ISBN 0 11 884486 5

Bibliographical reference

MATHERS, S J, HORTON, A, and BRISTOW, C R. 1993. Geology of the country around Diss. *Memoir of the British Geological Survey*, Sheet 175 (England and Wales).

Authors

S J Mathers, BSc
A Horton, BSc
British Geological Survey
Keyworth

C R Bristow, BSc, PhD
British Geological Survey
Exeter

Contributors

T E Lawson, BSc
formerly British Geological Survey

R J Wyatt, MBE
J A Zalasiewicz, BSc, PhD
British Geological Survey
Keyworth

D K Graham, BSc
British Geological Survey
Edinburgh

R A Monkhouse
British Geological Survey
Wallingford

Other publications of the Survey dealing with this and adjoining districts

BOOKS

British Regional Geology
East Anglia and adjoining areas (4th edition)

Memoirs
Sheet 161   Geology of the country around Norwich
Sheet 189   Geology of the country around Bury St Edmunds

Mineral Assessment Reports
No. 117   Sand and gravel resource sheet TM07 and part 08 (Redgrave, Suffolk)
No. 137   Sand and gravel resource sheet TM17 and part 18 (Diss, Norfolk)
No. 145   Sand and gravel resource sheets comprising parts of TM27, 28, 38 and 39 (Harleston and Bungay, Norfolk and Suffolk)

Well catalogues
Records of wells in the area around Norwich (Sheet 161)
Records of wells in the area of the New Series one-inch Geological Sheet 175 (Diss)
Records of wells in the area around Bury St Edmunds (Sheet 189)

MAPS

1:625 000
Solid geology (south sheet)
Quaternary geology (south sheet)

1:250 000
Solid geology, East Anglia
Quaternary geology, East Anglia
Aeromagnetic anomaly, East Anglia
Bouguer gravity anomaly, East Anglia

1:125 000
Hydrogeology, Northern East Anglia

1:50 000
Norwich (Sheet 161), Solid and Drift
Bury St Edmunds (Sheet 189), Solid and Drift

Printed in the UK for HMSO
Dd 295253 C8 9/93 531/3 12521

Geology of the country around Diss

The district described in this memoir lies largely within the county of Norfolk and is mainly rural in character. Widespread heavy clay loam soils are ideally suited to arable farming, and the principal settlements, Diss and Harleston, are market towns. The area is one of subdued relief and is almost entirely Drift-covered, much of it being a plateau of chalky Lowestoft Till.

Knowledge of the structure and stratigraphy of the Palaeozoic basement and the overlying Mesozoic sequence beneath the Chalk is based on boreholes drilled beyond the district. The upper part of this basement is probably composed of Siluro-Devonian sedimentary rocks. The succeeding Triassic rocks consist mainly of sandstones, which are probably of continental origin. A major marine transgression preceded deposition of the predominantly argillaceous, marine and, in part, richly fossiliferous Jurassic Lower Lias. Evidence of events during Middle and Upper Lias times is not preserved, and the brackish to marine beds of the Middle Jurassic rest non-sequentially upon the Lower Lias. These older Mesozoic sedimentary rocks die out south-eastwards, largely as a result of erosion and subsequent overstep by the overlying Cretaceous strata. These consist of a thin Carstone, overlain by the Gault and a thick Chalk sequence; only the Upper Cretaceous strata crop out in the district.

The oldest Quaternary deposits, the ?Red Crag and the Norwich Crag, are present in the eastern part of the district. They are known only from borehole sequences and are thought to have accumulated in a shallow-water, marine environment. The earliest Drift deposits are pre-Anglian fluvial sands and gravels. They are succeeded by glacial deposits, including tills, sands and gravels, and lacustrine silts and clays, derived from two distinct ice sheets. Younger, laminated, lacustrine silts and clays filling a depression at Hoxne were deposited under temperate conditions after the retreat of the ice; the locality has been defined as the type site of the Hoxnian Interglacial Stage. The subsequent history of the district has been one of progressive downcutting, with periods of deposition marked by river terrace and head deposits, and diverse Flandrian sediments.

The principal economic resources of the district are underground water derived mainly from the Chalk, and various sand and gravel deposits.

Cover photograph
The Mere, Diss [116 798], beneath which there are over 17 m of Flandrian mud deposits. View from the south. (A 15066)

CONTENTS

FIGURES

PLATES

TABLES

PREFACE

The district described in this memoir is sparsely populated and rural, and is largely given over to arable farming. The market towns of Diss and Harlestone provide the majority of services to this industry. The area is almost entirely covered with Drift deposits, the greater part being a gently undulating plateau composed of chalky till. The 1:50 000 geological map, which this account describes, will help agronomists who seek to make more effective use of their land by defining the distribution of the various drift deposits, which are the parent material for the major soil types.

There are few exposures in the district and the outcrops of all but the chalky till are largely confined to valley slopes. However, a mineral assess-ment programme has resulted in the definition of a sequence of drift deposits which can be compared with the well-documented successions in the Bury St Edmunds and Great Yarmouth areas. The deposits of Anglian age are recognised as the products of two distinct ice sheets, and older pre-Anglian fluvial sands and gravels are considered to represent the deposits of an early ancestral Thames river and its tributaries.

Although no borehole within the district has penetrated the basement, deep boreholes nearby, together with geophysical data, have enabled its form and structure to be inferred. Rocks of Siluro-Devonian age are presumed to be present in the upper part of the basement sequence, which is regarded as part of the London Platform stable block. Mesozoic forma-tions thin and pinch out from the north-west towards this block.

The most valuable economic resource of the district is underground water, which is tapped by a scattering of deep wells in the Chalk. The mineral assessment programme has shown some potential for sand and gravel resources, but at present they are worked on only a small scale. Clays formerly worked for brickmaking are no longer a viable resource.

The map shows that the district has a great range of Quaternary deposits, which contain a valuable record of rapid changes of climatic and depositional regimes during glacial and postglacial times, which in turn provide important insights into past global change.

Peter J Cook, DSc
Director

British Geological Survey
Keyworth
Nottingham
NG12 5GG

October 1992

HISTORY OF SURVEY OF THE DISS SHEET

Much of northern East Anglia was originally geologically surveyed in the 1870s and 1880s, and the results published in the Old Series One-inch Geological Map Series with accompanying memoirs. This district was covered by parts of the Quarter Sheets 50NW and NE, and 66 SW and SE, and their respective memoirs (Woodward, 1881; Bennett, 1884a, b; Whitaker and Dalton, 1887). Primary survey at the six-inch (1:10 560) and 1:10 000 scales was undertaken during the period 1978–86, mainly by Drs C R Bristow and J A Zalasiewicz and Messrs A Horton, T E Lawson, S J Mathers, C J Wilcox and R J Wyatt, with a small tract by M C McKeown and A Smith; these officers worked under the direction of Drs R A B Bazley, W A Read and R G Thurrell, Regional Geologists. The northern margin was mapped during the period 1965–69 by Dr F C Cox and Messrs M C McKeown and E G Poole, under the direction of Mr S C A Holmes, District Geologist.

The following is a list of 1:10 000- and 1:10 560-scale geological maps included wholly, or in part, in the area of the 1:50 000 Diss (175) geological sheet, with the initials of the surveying officers and the date of the survey for each map. The surveyors were: C R Bristow, F C Cox, A Horton, T E Lawson, S J Mathers, M C McKeown, E G Poole, A Smith, R J Wyatt, C J Wilcox and J A Zalasiewicz.

Manuscript copies of these maps have been deposited for public reference in the library of the British Geological Survey, Keyworth, Nottingham and in the British Geological Survey Information Point at the Geological Museum, Exhibition Road, South Kensington, London. They contain more detail than appears on the 1:50 000 map. National Grid dyeline copies are available, except for those marked thus †; open-file reports describing the local geology are available for maps marked with an asterisk.

TL 97 NE†	Hopton	CRB	1978
TL 98 NE†*	East Harling	JAZ, SJM	1985
TL 98 SE†	Riddlesworth	CJW	1979
TL 99 NE	Rockland All Saints	EGP	1965
TL 99 SE†*	Great Hockham	JAZ, SJM	1985
TM 07 NW*	Redgrave	CRB	1979
TM 07 NE*	Wortham	CRB	1979
TM 08 NW*	Kenninghall	SJM	1985
TM 08 NE*	Banham	JAZ	1985
TM 08 SW*	North Lopham	CJW	1979
TM 08 SE*	Bressingham	CJW	1980
TM 09 NW	Attleborough (northern)	EGP	1965
TM 09 NE	Besthorpe	EGP	1965
TM 09 SW*	Attleborough (southern)	MCM, AS	1985
TM 09 SE*	New Buckenham	SJM	1985
TM 17 NW*	Diss (southern)	AH	1979
TM 17 NE*	Hoxne	AH	1979
TM 18 NW*	Gissing	SJM	1985
TM 18 NE*	Pulham Market	JAZ	1985
TM 18 SW*	Diss (northern)	CJW	1980
TM 18 SE*	Dickleburgh	TEL	1979
TM 19 NW	Ashwellthorpe	MCM	1969
TM 19 NE	Flordon	FCC	1969
TM 19 SW*	Bunwell	SJM	1985
TM 19 SE*	Long Stratton	JAZ	1985
TM 27 NW*	Wingfield	AH	1980
TM 27 NE*	Fressingfield	AH	1980
TM 28 NW*	Pulham St Mary	TEL	1980
TM 28 NE*	Alburgh	TEL	1980
TM 28 SW*	Harleston	TEL	1980
TM 28 SE*	Mendham	TEL	1980
TM 29 NW	Saxlingham Nethergate	FCC	1969
TM 29 NE	Brooke	FCC	1969
TM 29 SW*	Hempnall	RJW	1980
TM 29 SE*	Topcroft	RJW	1980

ACKNOWLEDGEMENTS

NOTES

This account was initially drafted by Mr S J Mathers and later completed by Mr A Horton and Dr C R Bristow, and is based on the maps, field notes and open-file reports of the surveying officers. It incorporates stratigraphical data from boreholes drilled during the Survey's mineral assessment investigations of sand and gravel resources in parts of the district on behalf of the Department of the Environment. R A Monkhouse provided an account of the hydrogeology and water supply of the district. Mr D K Graham identified the Quaternary mollusca. M Abbot has provided information on the pre-Gault Mesozoic sequence. The memoir was edited by Mr R J Wyatt and Dr R G Thurrell.

The Survey gratefully acknowledges the information and assistance generously provided by various authorities, in particular, Norfolk County Council, Suffolk County Council and the Anglian Water Authority; also the willing co-operation of landowners, tenants and gravel pit operators during the execution of the fieldwork.

The survey of part of this district was supported by the Department of the Environment.

In this memoir, the word 'district' means the area included in the 1:50 000 geological sheet 175 (Diss).

Numbers in square brackets are National Grid references. They relate to the 100 km square TM except where otherwise indicated.

x

ONE

Introduction

The district lies in the heart of East Anglia, to the south of Norwich and east of Thetford, straddling the boundary between Norfolk and Suffolk. In common with much of East Anglia, its topography is subdued and forms a gently rolling landscape, rising locally to elevations in excess of 60 m above OD and falling to less than 20 m above OD in the major valleys (Figure 1). Much of the district is covered by a sheet of Lowestoft Till (chalky boulder clay) which produces a broad, fairly flat plateau generally in excess of 40 m above OD.

The drainage network is incised into the till plateau, with many of the major rivers following the courses of former glacial meltwater channels. In the south, the Little Ouse River drains westwards and the River Waveney eastwards

from a common source [044 789] north-west of Redgrave. Together, these two rivers form the boundary between Norfolk and Suffolk. The River Thet and its tributaries drain the north-western parts of the district, and the River Tas and its tributaries, which flow northwards to Norwich, drain the north-eastern part. Fens, the local name for marshes, were formerly widespread along the poorly drained stretches of these main river valleys; most have since been drained to produce farmland.

The district is mainly rural and is largely given over to arable farming. The soils are predominantly heavy clay loams developed on the till although, in the north-west, spreads of glacial sand and gravel give rise to lighter, sandy soils.

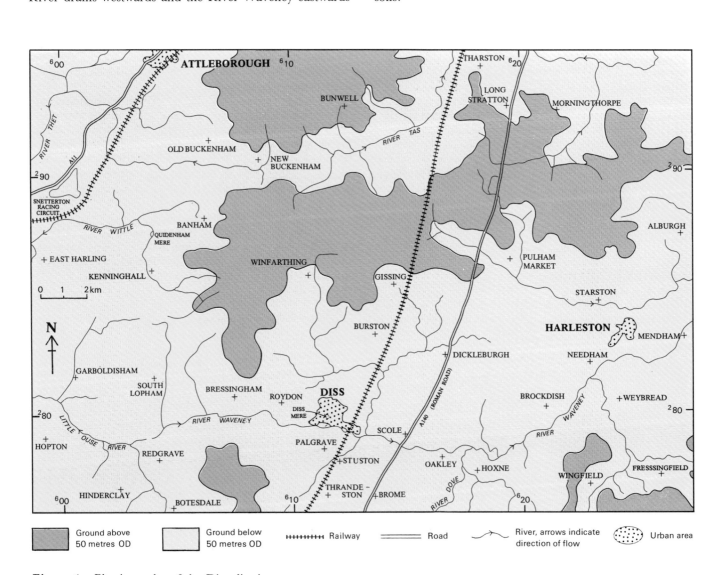

Figure 1   Physiography of the Diss district.

OUTLINE OF GEOLOGY

Quaternary deposits blanket most of the district and comprise two main divisions, the Norwich Crag and ?Red Crag, and the overlying Drift deposits.

Chalk underlies these Quaternary deposits throughout the district; it crops out only in the west. Knowledge of the structure and stratigraphy of the Palaeozoic basement and Mesozoic strata beneath the Chalk is based on deep boreholes drilled in adjacent areas, supplemented by regional geophysical data.

The Norwich Crag and ?Red Crag[1] comprise marine sediments laid down along the margin of the Southern North Sea Basin during early Pleistocene times. Over 50 m of these deposits are preserved in the south-east, where they infill part of a deep depression called the Stradbroke Basin; this depression extends south-westwards towards Sudbury (Bristow, 1983). The overlying Drift deposits have been laid down within the last million years. During this interval, the climate has oscillated between temperate (interglacial) and cold (glacial and periglacial) conditions, and the record of this alternation is the basis of the Quaternary stratigraphy (see inside front cover). Most of the Drift deposits in the district were probably formed during the colder climatic episodes; they comprise glacial sediments such as the Lowestoft Till (boulder clay) and outwash sediments, including glacial sand and gravel. The temperate or interglacial deposits comprise fluvial and lacustrine sediments, rich in organic material, and have a restricted areal distribution. Pollen analysis has been the most useful technique in attempting to determine their age. The correlation of much of the Drift sequence depends on its stratigraphical position relative to interglacial deposits, coupled with lithological and provenance studies. Direct dating using the radiocarbon technique can be applied only to sediments younger than about 40 000 years, that is to those from the Late Devensian or Flandrian.

PREVIOUS RESEARCH

Little geological research had been carried out previously within the district, largely because so much of it is formed of a monotonous spread of Lowestoft Till with few geological sections or exposures, either natural or man-made. Much of the stratigraphy is based on comparisons and correlations with adjacent areas, rather than on evidence from within the district.

The original geological survey of the district at the scale of 1:63 360 was undertaken in 1881–84, and published as Quarter Sheets (50NW, 50NE, 66SW and 66SE) with accompanying memoirs (Woodward, 1881; Bennett, 1884a; b; Whitaker and Dalton, 1887) describing the stratigraphy.

Brickpits near Hoxne have been extensively studied since 1797, when Frere (1800) noted the discovery of palaeolithic hand-axes in gravelly deposits (head gravel) overlying brick clay (interglacial silt and clay). The latter has been extensively studied by West (1956), and the archaeology and stratigraphy of the site has been summarised by Wymer (1983). The Oakley Park Brickpit [1745 7665] was adopted as the type site for the Hoxnian Stage of the Quaternary (Mitchell et al., 1973).

Other studies relate to the evolution of the River Waveney since the Anglian glaciation. Organic interglacial deposits of Ipswichian age have been identified by Sparks and West (1968) from a site at Wortwell, a few hundred metres beyond the eastern boundary of the district. More recently, Coxon (1979, 1984) has investigated the chronology and evolution of the Waveney drainage system and assigned provisional ages to the river terrace deposits.

In recent years, knowledge of the distribution and stratigraphy of the Quaternary of the southern part of the district has been considerably improved following aggregate assessment surveys carried out by the British Geological Survey (Auton, 1982; Wilcox and Stanczyszyn, 1983; Auton et al., 1985). The stratigraphy and distribution of the Quaternary deposits at depth in the northern half of the district, however, remain poorly known.

The stratigraphical sequence of the Quaternary deposits (see inside front cover) is, where possible, related to the stages proposed by Mitchell et al. (1973), taking account of the modifications suggested by Funnell et al. (1979), Mayhew (1985) and Mayhew and Stuart (1986).

---

1 Crag is a name used colloquially in East Anglia for shelly sand.

TWO

Palaeozoic rocks

The entire district is underlain at a few hundred metres depth by a basement composed of Palaeozoic rocks (Figure 2). This basement is part of the east–west-aligned London Platform that underlies much of central and eastern England. The massif is composed of Precambrian and Palaeozoic rocks, most of which were deformed by the Caledonian orogeny and subsequently formed the foreland to the Variscan fold belt of southern Britain. The massif has remained a tectonically stable basement block ever since.

Although no borehole within the district has reached the basement, several deep boreholes nearby, combined with geophysical data, enable its form and structure to be inferred. The general structural trend of the deeper basement rocks is WNW–ESE, a direction which is common in most of northern East Anglia and probably also in adjoining parts of the North Sea. Within the district, one conspicuous

magnetic anomaly indicates a body with this trend, probably made up of rocks of Precambrian age, at a depth of 4 to 5 km below the surface. The basement was subjected to prolonged erosion during Upper Palaeozoic and earliest Mesozoic times; its upper surface slopes gently north-east at about one-third of a degree, falling from 230 m below OD in the south-west to about 400 m below OD in the north-east (Figure 2; Cox et al., 1989, fig.3a).

Throughout the district, the basement rocks are overlain unconformably by Mesozoic strata. The upper part of the basement in the west is thought to be composed of Siluro-Devonian sedimentary rocks, similar to those proved in four deep boreholes nearby, namely Rocklands [TL 9952 9670], Breckles [TL 9551 9469], Great Ellingham [0262 9847] (Cox et al., 1989) and Four Ashes [0223 7186] (Bristow, 1980). These Devonian deposits comprise weakly metamorphosed

Figure 2 Sketch map of the solid geology of the Diss and adjacent districts, with the locations of deep boreholes.

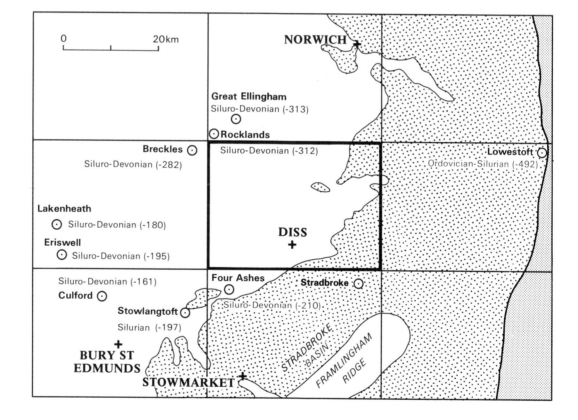

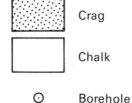

Crag

Chalk

⊙ Borehole

-282 Depth in metres below Ordnance Datum of pre-Permian surface

sandstones, siltstones and shales, commonly inclined at 20° to 30°; the siltstones and shales are cleaved. In the east, Silurian sedimentary rocks may crop out at the upper surface of the basement (British Geological Survey, 1985, map 1). In the south-west, Silurian sedimentary rocks have been proved beneath the Mesozoic cover at Stowlangtoft [TL 9475 6682] (Bristow, 1990).

There is evidence at shallower depth for the existence of structures trending north-north-east, including, in the south-east of the district, the northern end of the ridge of Chalk which separates thicker sequences of Crag farther south. Geophysical results suggest that this feature is a horst-like structure, bounded by faults that extend down into the basement (Cornwell, 1985).

THREE

Mesozoic rocks

TRIASSIC AND JURASSIC

Very close to the north-western corner of the district, Triassic and Jurassic sedimentary rocks have been proved resting on basement in the deep boreholes at Rocklands [TL 9952 9670], Breckles [TL 9551 9469] and Great Ellingham [0262 9847]. These deposits probably extend beneath the adjacent north-western parts of the district (Figure 3; Cox et al., 1989, fig.4).

The generalised sequence shown inside the front cover is based on the cored sequence proved in the Great Ellingham Borehole (Figure 2). Additional information is available from the geophysical logs of this borehole and the others at Rocklands and Breckles which were not cored.

The Triassic strata comprise horizontally bedded sandstone with thin siltstone and mudstone beds. At Great Ellingham, the basal 15 m contain pebbles of rounded red and green siltstone and mudstone, and angular flakes of mudstone (?Devonian). These beds are overlapped by the Jurassic (Figure 3), as over other parts of the London Platform to the west, but geophysical evidence to the east of the district and beneath the North Sea suggests that the Triassic strata may have extended much farther south at one stage and now pinch out beneath the Carstone unconformity, farther south-east than the Lower Lias in places (M Abbott, personal communication).

A long period of erosion preceded deposition of the transgressive Lower Lias, which, at Great Ellingham, commenced during the *Echioceras raricostatum* Zone; zones younger than the overlying *Uptonia jamesoni* Zone have been eroded there. In the Diss district, deposition probably commenced at a slightly later stage in the transgression. The basal Lias at Great Ellingham comprises fossiliferous mudstones rich in shell debris with pebbles of phosphate, quartz, limestone and chert, and with limonitic ooliths. It is overlain by smooth mudstones with thin ironstones and cementstones. Similar beds probably persist into the present district. The Middle and Upper Lias were probably never deposited locally.

The base of the Middle Jurassic at Great Ellingham has been taken at a depth of 293.98 m (Gallois, *in* Cox et al., 1989, p.33), but could be drawn at about 292.80 m. The lithology of the 1.18 m of strata between these depths, comprising two beds of pale grey, slightly ochreous mottled, silty mudstone with sphaerosiderite, separated by a smooth-textured mudstone, is identical to the underlying Lias, except for its pallid colour which results from weathering associated with the pre-Middle Jurassic land surface. It is possible that this interval represents a soil horizon (seatearth) developed in the uppermost Lower Lias. The beds above about 292.84 m are undoubtedly Middle Jurassic and comprise a pale grey, muddy siltstone of seatearth type, overlain by dark purplish grey, very silty mudstone with carbonised wood fragments and pyritic rootlets. They are very similar to the Freshwater Sequence of the Upper Estuarine 'Series' of

Peterborough (Horton, 1989). The youngest Middle Jurassic strata at Great Ellingham comprise calcareous mudstones and marls with bivalves, rhynchonellids, echinoids, crinoids and fish debris, overlain by a hard sparry and micritic limestone. Although previously classified with the Upper Estuarine 'Series' (Gallois, *in* Cox et al., 1989), they more closely resemble the Blisworth Limestone of the outcrop area, although of a more argillaceous facies. These beds are overlain at 288.80 m by the Carstone, although geophysical evidence from the Breckles Borehole indicates that thin, possibly Upper Jurassic mudstone may intervene in the extreme north-west of the district (M Abbott, personal communication).

The Mesozoic strata die out south-eastwards, largely as a result of erosion and subsequent overstep by the overlying Cretaceous strata, which rest directly on the basement just south of the district in the Four Ashes Borehole [0223 7186] (Bristow, 1980).

CRETACEOUS

A thick sequence of Cretaceous sedimentary rocks is present throughout the district, but only the Upper Chalk crops out at the surface. The beds dip gently eastwards at about one-third of a degree, with the thickest preserved sequence of about 330 m occurring in the east.

The strata comprise a thin Lower Cretaceous succession of Carstone overlain by Gault, followed by the much thicker Upper Cretaceous Chalk. No borehole within the district penetrates the entire Cretaceous sequence. However, the deep boreholes and outcrops in the adjoining Norwich (Sheet 161), Thetford (Sheet 174), Bury St Edmunds (Sheet 189) and Eye (Sheet 190) districts (Figure 2) permit a confident prediction of the sequence (Figure 3).

Carstone

The Carstone has been proved in the Rocklands (9.7 m), Breckles (8.8 m) and Great Ellingham (6.7 m) boreholes. To the south, the Four Ashes Borehole proved only 0.4 m (Morter, *in* Bristow, 1980; Gallois and Morter, 1982). This suggests that the Carstone is present at least in the west of the district, and that it thins southwards (Figure 3).

The Carstone proved in these boreholes, and at outcrop in north-west Norfolk, comprises brown, yellowish brown and greenish grey, medium- to coarse-grained sands that include pebbles of quartz and quartzite, and abundant ooliths of limonite and limonitised 'chamosite'. The deposit is commonly bioturbated. The Carstone contains derived Aptian fossils especially in its basal beds, together with an indigenous fauna of brachiopods and ammonites (Casey and Gallois, 1973) of the Lower Albian, *Leymeriella tardefurcata* and *Douvilleiceras mammillatum* zones. Gallois and Morter (1982) have suggested that the thin Carstone deposits

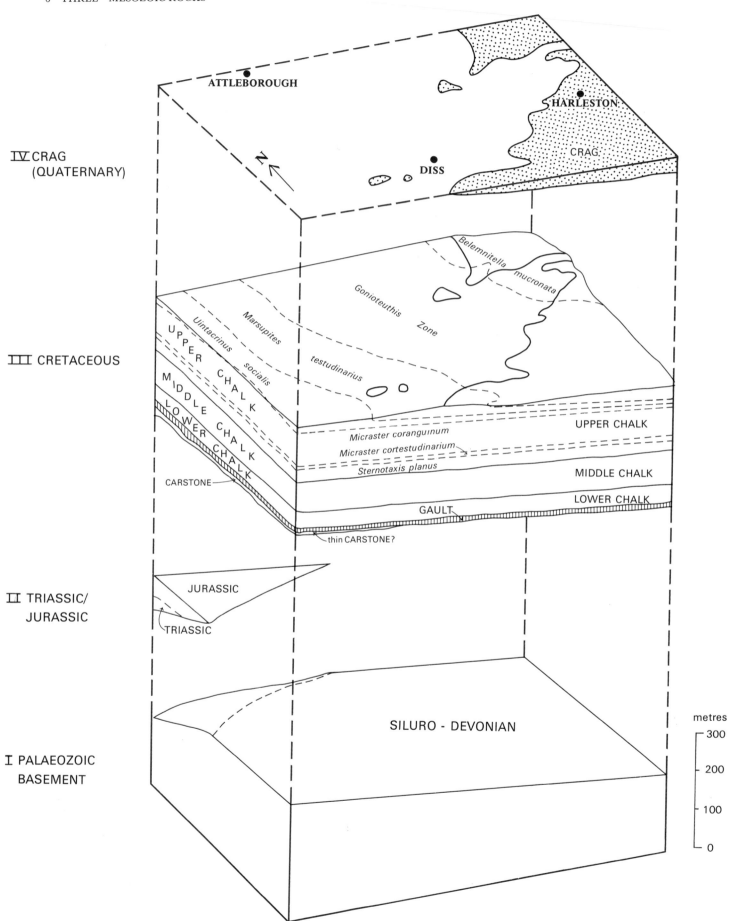

IV CRAG (QUATERNARY)

III CRETACEOUS

II TRIASSIC/ JURASSIC

I PALAEOZOIC BASEMENT

ATTLEBOROUGH

HARLESTON

N

DISS

CRAG

Belemnitella mucronata

Gonioteuthis Zone

Uintacrinus socialis

Marsupites testudinarius

UPPER CHALK

MIDDLE CHALK

LOWER CHALK

CARSTONE

Micraster coranguinum

Micraster cortestudinarium

Sternotaxis planus

UPPER CHALK

MIDDLE CHALK

LOWER CHALK

GAULT

thin CARSTONE?

JURASSIC

TRIASSIC

SILURO - DEVONIAN

metres
300
200
100
0

Figure 3 Exploded block diagram of the solid geology of the district.

preserved in the north-west of the district formed as a near-shore extension of the much thicker sand sequence preserved in the Hunstanton area, interpreted by them as an offshore bar.

Gault

The presence of the Gault at depth throughout the district is inferred from boreholes in adjoining areas. Recorded thicknesses are 17.3 m at Four Ashes, 13.5 m at Stowlangtoft, 11.3 m at Great Ellingham and 12.5 m at both Rocklands and Breckles.

The Gault comprises grey, variably silty mudstones and calcareous mudstones, which are commonly bioturbated. Parts of the sequence contain an abundant fauna, notably bivalves (inoceramids), hoplitid ammonites, and belemnites such as *Neohibolites*. Rhythmic units have been recognised within the deposits (Gallois and Morter, 1982). Each unit is 1 to 2 m thick and rests typically on an erosion surface. A basal layer of phosphate pebbles, worn belemnites and shell fragments is overlain by mudstones which become progressively less silty and more calcareous towards the top of the unit. By a combination of lithology and fauna, nineteen beds have been recognised in the Gault over much of Norfolk. The lowest beds of the sequence are present in the Great Ellingham Borehole where the Gault appears to rest conformably upon Carstone. At Stowlangtoft, Beds 1 and 2 appear to be missing, and Beds 3 to 5 are represented by 0.66 m of dark, densely burrowed shelly mudstone. At the base of this mudstone is a 2 cm-thick bed of pyritic glauconitic clay with belemnites. In the Four Ashes Borehole, however, the lowermost beds (Nos. 1–4) are either absent or condensed into a thin layer of Carstone lithofacies. In the Clare Borehole [TL 7834 4536] farther south, beds 1 to 10 are absent. Thus the beds comprising the Gault progressively overstep southwards onto the Palaeozoic basement.

To the north of the district, the Gault becomes attenuated and passes into the 1.5 m-thick Red Chalk of north-west Norfolk. The Gault and Red Chalk accumulated in a shallow, protected, low-energy, marine embayment bounded to the north by a relict Carstone shoal around Hunstanton. The lithological difference between these deposits reflects two separate sources of clay-grade sediment; the grey Gault was derived from the Palaeozoic massif to the south and the Red Chalk from the Carstone shoal to the north, which accounts for its characteristic colour (Gallois and Morter, 1982).

Chalk

Chalk is a very pure, micritic limestone composed largely of the disaggregated skeletons of planktonic coccolithophorid algae. The debris generally occurs as individual laths and plates a few microns across; more exceptionally, rings of laths called coccoliths are preserved. Scattered macrofossils occur throughout, but are abundant only in distinct layers; aragonitic forms are only rarely preserved. The main macrofossil groups represented are sponges, terebratulid and rhynchonellid brachiopods, gastropods, bivalves, ammonites, belemnites, echinoids and crinoids. Microfossils include foraminifera and ostracods. The strata range in age from the Cenomanian to Campanian.

Much of the Upper Chalk and the higher part of the Middle Chalk contain flint nodules, which are commonly distributed in layers. The flint is almost pure silica. It originated from the dissolution of sponge spicules and other siliceous material, the resulting solution migrating through the chalk sediment and precipitating silica at sites rich in organic material such as burrow infills. The mineral was probably precipitated initially as opaline silica which, subsequently, underwent transformation to form chalcedonic quartz.

The Chalk probably accumulated as an ooze in a subtropical sea of normal salinity in water depths between 100 and 600 m (Hancock, 1975). The general absence of clastic sediment indicates a lack of erosion of the adjacent contemporary landmasses.

At the western extremity of the district, the Chalk is about 240 m thick. It thickens eastwards downdip as progressively higher beds are preserved, to reach a maximum of some 330 m. The Chalk outcrops are confined to the western half of the district, principally around Kenninghall [038 861] and East Harling [TL 994 866]. Whilst several boreholes prove thick Chalk sequences, the most reliable and detailed information about the succession comes from the Stowlangtoft Borehole, from electrical resistivity logs of two boreholes beyond the district (west of East Harling and near Thetford), and from surface exposures in the adjacent Thetford (174) and Bury St Edmunds (189) districts, details of which are given by Hewitt (1924, 1935), Brydone (1931, 1932) (summarised in a compilation by Peake and Hancock, 1961) and Bristow (1990).

The Chalk can be divided into three lithostratigraphical units, namely the Lower, Middle and Upper Chalk (Figure 4). The Lower Chalk comprises up to 45 m of flintless, grey and white, marly chalk. It is overlain by about 60 m of Middle Chalk comprising white chalk with thin marl seams and a few flints. The base of the Upper Chalk is marked by chalk containing large flints, the Brandon Flint 'Series', which, in the past, was traditionally placed in the upper part of the Middle Chalk at the top of the *Terebratulina lata* Zone (see Ward, Burland and Gallois, 1968). However, the 'Series' equates with the flinty beds at the base of the *Sternotaxis plana* Zone in southern England, i.e. the flints used by the Geological Survey as a criterion for mapping the base of the Upper Chalk in the North Downs and adjacent areas (Mortimore and Wood, 1986). The Chalk Rock, which falls in the middle of the *plana* Zone in expanded sequences, was once the commonly accepted mappable base for the Upper Chalk (see Worssam and Taylor, 1969) and it was the boundary adopted on the 1:50 000 Cambridge (188) and Bury St Edmunds (189) geological sheets. The Upper Chalk is up to 220 m thick and consists of flint-rich white chalk.

At Stowlangtoft, the Lower Chalk is 48 m thick (Bristow, 1990); thicknesses in other boreholes near the district are given by electrical resistivity logs, as follows: Four Ashes (42.4 m), Rocklands (38.1 m) and Breckles (43.9 m). The

Figure 4 Cretaceous stratigraphy of the district.

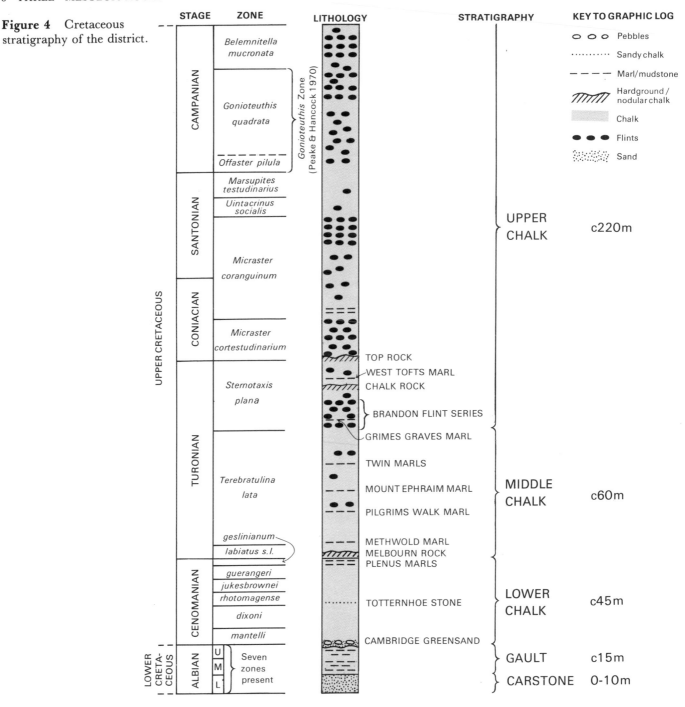

Cambridge Greensand, the basal member of the sequence, is 1.45 m thick at Stowlangtoft and rests unconformably on Gault. The Cambridge Greensand comprises a highly fossiliferous, sandy, glauconitic, calcareous siltstone with a basal layer of phosphate pebbles; it is a condensed bed and contains many derived Upper Albian fossils as well as indigenous Cenomanian forms dominated by terebratulid brachiopods and bivalves, notably *Aucellina* (Morter and Wood, 1983). Within the overlying massive, marly, off-white to grey Lower Chalk, there is another condensed bed, the Totternhoe Stone. This is a silty, 'gritty' chalk which rests on a pronounced erosion surface and contains glaucon-

itised and phosphatised pebbles at its base. The uppermost metre or so of the Lower Chalk is an alternation of thin marls and marly chalks called the Plenus Marls after the belemnite *Actinocamax plenus*. This bed is a useful marker since it can be readily recognised on most electrical resistivity borehole logs (Murray, 1986).

The Middle Chalk is probably about 60 m thick; 67 m were proved at Stowlangtoft and 71 m at Four Ashes. It comprises the thin biozone of the bivalve *Mytiloides labiatus* s.l. and the much thicker overlying zone of the brachiopod *Terebratulina lata*. The basal bed is the Melbourn Rock, a hard, poorly fossiliferous, nodular chalk up to 3 m thick.

This is overlain by several metres of chalk rich in whole and fragmented bivalves (*Mytiloides*). The succeeding part of the Middle Chalk contains sporadic layers of flint in the upper part and several marl seams, generally less than 0.1 m thick (Figure 4). Individual seams are extensive and can be correlated effectively using electrical resistivity logs (Murray, 1986).

The Upper Chalk attains its maximum preserved thickness of about 220 m beneath the eastern margin of the district; its base is taken at the base of the Brandon Flint 'Series', which comprises about 10 m of flint-rich chalk characterised by large nodular and tabular flints up to 0.3 m thick (Skertchley, 1879; Mortimore and Wood, 1986). The Chalk Rock lies close above and consists of one or more thin beds of hard nodular chalk with a rich fauna of ammonites, gastropods and bivalves. It is succeeded by about 10 m of firm white chalk, which are capped by a mineralised, glauconitised hardground known as the Top Rock (Figure 4); the latter is a strongly condensed sequence representing the lower part of the *Micraster cortestudinarium* Zone. The succeeding soft, flint-rich chalk spans the higher part of the *M. cortestudinarium* Zone and the *M. coranguinum* Zone; the two overlying crinoid zones, *Uintacrinus socialis* and *Marsupites testudinarius* are, however, characterised by chalk with relatively little flint. Chalk of the succeeding *Gonioteuthis* (undivided) and *Belemnitella mucronata* zones has a subdrift crop over most of the central and eastern part of the district. There is no detail available from the small outcrops within this tract.

DETAILS

Fossils of *socialis* Zone age have been recorded from a pit [001 868] and a well [TL 997 858] near East Harling (Hewitt, 1935, p.25). At the East Harling limekiln [0447 8762], on the Quidenham road, Hewitt (1935) saw 2.4 m of soft chalk with a line of smooth-coated and irregular flints near the top; fossils were scarce, but plates of *Uintacrinus*, together with *Serpula ampullacea*, *S. plana*, *Kingena lima*,

Neithea quinquecostata, *Ostrea boucheroni*, *O. incurva*, *Pecten* (*Chlamys*) *cretosus*, *Septifer lineatus* and *Cidaris serrifera*, were found. Brydone (1932, p.159) referred to the reported common occurrence of *Actinocamax* of the *verus* group near East Harling, and to his own finds of specimens of *A. verus* and a possible *Uintacrinus westphalicus* in a pit [TL 9931 8316] on Garboldisham Heath. He suggested (1932, p.158) that the boundary between the *coranguinum* and *socialis* zones ran through the pit. Brydone (1932, p.158) also recorded common *U. westphalicus* near Hall Farm, Garboldisham [TL 999 829].

In the extreme south-west of the district [0077 7602], chalk of presumed *socialis* Zone age can be found in the bottom of a ditch 600 m north-east of Dairy Farm.

There are two old chalk pits [0345 7627 and 0363 7635] west of Broom Hills. Bennett (1884b, p.5) recorded 4.2 m of soft chalk with a few flints, overlain by gravel in the eastern pit. Brydone (1932, p.159) noted that brachials of *Uintacrinus* were common in this pit. The old chalk pit [0481 7612] at Botesdale was briefly described by Bennett (1884b, p.5). There, 6 m of marly and rubbly chalk were overlain by patches of gravel. A line of flints in the lower part of the pit revealed an 'anticlinal fold', with one limb dipping at 45°. This fold is probably a cryoturbation structure. Brydone (1932) visited this pit, but found no fossil. At Butts Plantation, Chalk with *Inoceramus* fragments was exposed in a ditch [0430 7678]. Chalk was formerly worked in three pits [0547 7847; 0559 7865; 0567 7814] in the Redgrave area. In the last pit, Brydone (1932, p.159) found common brachials of *Uintacrinus*.

Chalk of *testudinarius* Zone age was formerly exposed in a pit at Uphall. There, Hewitt (1935, p.25) recorded 1 m of chalk, under 3 m of 'cover', of which 2.1 m was 'rearranged' chalk [0134 8423]. The chalk was very soft and with no in-situ flints. Plates of *Marsupites* were found just above the solid chalk (see also Brydone, 1931, p.116).

In the large pit [0885 7920] north-east of Wortham Hall, soft white chalk with flints was still visible in 1979. It is presumably from this pit that Brydone (1932, p.160) found plates of *Marsupites*. His reference to a chalk pit at Manor Farm, Wortham [0745 7980], may be an error for Wortham Hall, as there is no outcrop of chalk at the former locality.

Chalk with *Marsupites* and *Ditrupula triminghamiensis* was recorded by Brydone (1932, p.160) at Stuston [?1295 7875] and chalk of *Offaster pilula* Zone age occurs at the Banham limekiln [065 878].

FOUR

Post-Cretaceous structure

At the end of the Cretaceous period, widespread marine deposition ceased and there was a period of uplift and gentle folding. The upper part of the Chalk was eroded, and where overlain by Lower London Tertiary deposits to the south of the district, the various zones of the Chalk are truncated by the later deposits, although in individual sections no angular discordance can be seen. The Diss district probably lay close to the northern margin of the Tertiary sedimentary basin, and the only evidence for these deposits is provided by the glauconite-coated flints derived from the Bullhead Bed at the base of the Thanet Beds, which were incorporated in the base of the Crag (Bristow, 1983). It is possible that some of the Crag sands were also derived from the Thanet Beds (Bristow, 1983).

The Plio-Pleistocene Crag deposits are particularly thick within the south-west-trending Stradbroke Basin, the north-ern part of which extends into the south-eastern part of the district. This basin, and others in East Anglia, are considered by Bristow (1983, fig.1) to be fault-bounded, the faulting having been associated with uplift during the Miocene. The residual gravity anomaly map of the region (Cornwell, 1985) indicates linear structures at depth which are coincident with the basin margins. Mathers and Zalasiewicz (1988), however, do not fully accept the fault-bounded nature of the Crag basins and suggest that sea-bed scour could produce such marked relief.

Following the deposition of the Crag, an eastward down-warping of the coastal Crag sequence towards the North Sea Basin took place, with a compensatory uplift in the inland areas of southern East Anglia (Mathers and Zalasiewicz, 1988).

FIVE

Quaternary solid

Norwich Crag and ?Red Crag

The term Crag has been widely used in East Anglia to describe shelly sands of Plio-Pleistocene age. It is present beneath Quaternary deposits throughout the southern to north-eastern parts of the district (Figure 2). The subsurface distribution is based on borehole evidence; this is of good quality within the areas covered by the BGS mineral assessment reports (Auton, 1982; Wilcox and Stanczyscyn, 1983; and Auton et al., 1985), but is conjectural in the north-east, where there are no detailed borehole records and where it is difficult to distinguish Crag, particularly when weathered, from the overlying Drift deposits. The only outcrops are north-east of Redgrave [068 792 and 075 793] where they form part of a more extensive subcrop beneath drift, less than 3 m thick. A second subdrift occurrence lies north-east of Wortham, and a third, with about 1 m of Crag, has been tentatively identified from the evidence of a single borehole [0836 9100] north-west of New Buckenham. The presence of these outliers indicates the former greater westward extent of the Crag deposits.

The Crag rests unconformably upon the Chalk, and its upper surface is erosional and uneven due to channelling beneath the Drift deposits. Nevertheless, there is a general increase in thickness south-eastward, with possibly at least 60 m being present near Fressingfield [2603 7730]. This area forms the northern part of a complex, shallow depression in the surface of the Upper Chalk, the Stradbroke Basin, the axis of which lies to the south-east of the present district. In the south, near Brome, and in the north-east, around Top-croft, the Crag is probably less than 20 m thick.

No borehole has proved a thick, complete sequence in the Crag. Lithological information derived from boreholes comes from: i) the zone of pinch out, where only the lower parts of the formation were penetrated and ii) downdip, where only the upper parts were drilled. The results of grain size analysis of some 650 samples collected from the mineral assessment programme boreholes is given in Table 1.

The assessment areas extend southwards considerably beyond the Diss district, but these results show that the Crag is relatively uniform and consists of a fine- to medium-grained sand. The sands are commonly glauconitic and micaceous and are usually medium to dark greenish grey or greyish green when fresh. They are generally oxidised, iron stained and leached to ochreous hues above the water table. Secondary iron pan commonly occurs at this level. The sands are shelly, particularly in areas of thick development. Loosely cemented, shelly sandstones may be present. Discrete laminae of clay, silty clay or clayey silt may occur within the sands.

In the Redgrave area, pebbles of flint, quartzite and quartz, and phosphatic nodules with ironstone and iron pan occur towards the base of the Crag. At outcrop, to the west, south-west and north-east of the district, glauconite-coated flints are present in the basal bed of the Crag (Bristow, 1983, 1986). These flints are thought by Bristow (1983) to have been derived from the Bullhead Bed at the base of the Thanet Beds. The base of the Crag is not exposed in the district, but glauconite-coated flints have been noted in the Kesgrave Sands and Gravels at a locality [0349 7502] immediately south of it.

Table 1 Mean grading characteristics of the Crag.

Mineral assessment report area[1]	Mean grading percentages						Number of samples
	Fines	Sand			Gravel		
	$-\frac{1}{16}$ mm	$+\frac{1}{16}$ to $-\frac{1}{4}$ mm	$+\frac{1}{4}$ to -1 mm	$+1$ to -4 mm	$+4$ to 16 mm	$+16$ to 64 mm	
Redgrave TM07	17	81			2		203
		56	23	2	1	1	
Diss TM17	7	92			1		247
		48	42	2	?	?	
Harleston[2] TM27	10	87			3		? (201 samples in total)
		data available but not presented in this form					

1 The area covered by the reports extends beyond the Diss sheet.
2 These gradings are for samples considered to be of value as a mineral; i.e. they do not contain glauconite or an excessive amount of shell debris (Auton et al., 1985).

Lenses of gravel occur in the lower part of the Crag in the south-eastern and north-eastern parts of the district. A borehole [2289 8415] near Starston proved only the basal Crag sequence, which consisted of 1.5 m of gravel with glauconite-coated, black flint pebbles (53 per cent by weight), angular flints (30 per cent), some vein quartz and quartzite pebbles, and shell fragments. Up to 3.0 m of fine- to medium-grained, well-sorted, slightly micaceous, flat- and cross-bedded sand with rare clay laminae were seen beneath Drift in the eastern face of Morningthorpe Gravel Pit [220 944], north of Morningthorpe. Strings of well-rounded flint pebbles coalesce into a thick lens of bedded gravel at one point (see below).

The Crag within the district is shown provisionally to include Red Crag on the published map, but this can only be confirmed when detailed faunal studies of the sequence are available. The presence of the Red Crag is inferred from the results of the Stradbroke Borehole, about 2 km to the south of the district (Figure 2) which lies within the Stradbroke Basin, a complex shallow north-east to south-west elongated basin which extends from Stradbroke through Stowmarket towards Sudbury (Bristow, 1983). The lower part of the Crag sequence in the borehole consisted of shelly, glauconitic, moderately sorted, medium- to coarse-grained sands with subordinate clay layers and some thin pebbly seams. Pollen and foraminiferal assemblages indicate the presence of the Pre-Ludhamian and Ludhamian stages (Beck et al., 1972), which biostratigraphically correspond to the Red Crag (*sensu* Funnell and West, 1977). The upper part of the sequence commonly comprises micaceous, well-sorted, fine- to medium-grained sands, which are shelly and clayey in part. These resemble the sediments classified as Norwich Crag and may belong to the Bramertonian Stage (Funnell et al., 1979). They probably extend northward to Harleston where they immediately underlie the Drift deposits, and thence to Hempnall where they are co-extensive with the Norwich Crag on the Norwich (161) Sheet. The Crag deposits west of Hoxne occur within the Kettlebaston Basin (Bristow, 1983); their faunas, collected from places south-west of the present district, are of Red Crag rather than Norwich Crag aspect.

The faunas within the Crag are very varied, but are dominated by gastropods and bivalves. Typical species include the bivalves *Glycimeris*, *Arctica*, *Cardium*, *Mya* and *Mytilus*, and the gastropod *Neptunea*. The faunas of the Red Crag indicate conditions slightly warmer than those in which the Norwich Crag accumulated, and also slightly warmer than those of the present day (Harmer, 1900, 1902).

The Crag was laid down along the western margin of the Southern North Sea Basin during the interval 2.5 to about 1.0 Ma ago. The Red Crag was probably deposited in a shallow, tidally dominated, temperate shelf sea (Boatman, 1977; Dixon, 1979; Zalasiewicz and Mathers, 1985). The overlying Norwich Crag accumulated nearer shore in shallow-marine and intertidal conditions (West and Norton, 1974; Zalasiewicz and Mathers, 1985).

Westleton Beds

Gravels with a clean sand matrix, which are characterised by abundant rounded flint pebbles and a small percentage of angular flints, and quartz and quartzite pebbles, have been proved at depth in seven boreholes in the Harleston–Fressingfield area, in the extreme south-east of the district. The maximum thickness of 3.7 m was recorded in a borehole [2420 8243] south of Harleston. In a borehole [2289 8415] near Starston, similar gravels overlie 1.5 m of probable Crag; the latter is comparable in lithology to the overlying unit, except that the rounded black flint pebbles are glauconite coated and the sand matrix contains shell debris. Pebbles of quartz, quartzite and rare phosphate, and angular flints, occur in the top of the Crag in other boreholes in the Starston area.

In the north-west of the district, an old gravel pit at Mill Farm [2086 9494], north-north-east of Stratton St Michael, revealed up to 4.0 m of well-rounded, bedded, densely packed, dominantly flint (95 per cent) gravel, with subordinate quartz and quartzite (<5 per cent), beneath glacial sand and gravel. A thick lens of similar gravel was observed within 3.0 m of sands assigned to the Norwich Crag at the base of the east face of Morningthorpe Gravel Pit [220 944] nearby (Wyatt, 1981).

Auton et al. (1985) regarded these gravels as drift and included them as the basal member of the Beccles Beds. Lithologically, however, they are comparable to the Westleton Beds of the type area near Southwold, Suffolk (Hey, 1967), which have been interpreted as high-energy, marginal beach deposits. They have been included (West and Norton, 1974; Funnel et al., 1979) within an extensive suite of sediments laid down during the Bramertonian Stage, and thus form part of the Norwich Crag. Zalasiewicz (*in* Gibbard and Zalasiewicz, 1988, fig.3) considers that they may belong to the younger Baventian Stage.

SIX

Quaternary drift—Pre-Anglian

The sequence and distribution of the drift deposits shown on the published Diss 1:50 000 sheet is a compromise between i) what can be mapped economically at outcrop, a function of degree of exposure, the thickness and lithology of the units defined and the topography, ii) what can be depicted on a 1:50 000 scale map and iii) what can be gleaned from boreholes in which the description of lithologies can range from the 'sand and gravel' of drillers' logs to the detailed grain size and pebble-count data included in BGS mineral assessment borehole logs.

The lithostratigraphy of the older drift deposits is shown in Table 2, which equates the terms used on the 1:50 000 map with those used on 1:10 000 maps and their associated reports. The survey of the Diss Sheet occurred in two stages. Firstly, the survey of the southern and eastern parts (1979–80) was undertaken as the first part of an assessment of the sand and gravel resources of the Waveney valley and its environs. This was followed by an extensive borehole investigation of the drift deposits, enabling the development of a detailed lithostratigraphical classification (Auton, 1982; Wilcox and Stanczyszyn, 1983), which was enhanced during the final stages of the sand and gravel assessment (Auton et al., 1985). The field survey of the northern and western parts of the Diss Sheet was completed in 1985.

Initially the sand and gravel deposits were divided into an older fluviatile suite and a younger glacigenic suite. The older sediments comprise sands and gravels with a significant proportion of quartz, quartzite and flint pebbles (Table 3); they rest directly on the Norwich Crag or Chalk. These deposits crop out in the Redgrave and Oakley areas, and are equated with the Kesgrave Sands and Gravels (Rose and Allen, 1977). A second unit, the Ingham Sand and Gravel, of comparable, but distinct lithology, and about the same age, was subsequently proved in boreholes in the south-eastern parts of the district. Over much of the district, these fluviatile deposits are buried beneath the glacigenic sediments.

In the first area to be surveyed, around Palgrave, all glacigenic sands and gravels were classified as glacial sand and gravel, a usage that is followed on the 1:50 000 sheet. Subsequently, in the Diss area, it was possible to divide them into two lithological types: i) mainly flint-rich sands and gravels which are thought to be of a north-eastern provenance, and ii) chalk-flint-rich sands and gravels, which are

Table 2 Lithostratigraphy of the older drift deposits and the relationship of the glacial sand and gravel depicted on the map to these units.

Stage/provenance		North-western area	Redgrave area	Diss area	Harleston area	Great Yarmouth sheet
Hoxnian		—	—	Interglacial silt and clay (Hoxne Beds)	—	—
Anglian	North-western provenance	**Lowestoft Till** + **Glacial sand and gravel** (chalk-flint-rich) + **Glacial silt and clay** (channel-fill deposits)				Lowestoft (Till) Formation
	North-eastern Provenance	**Glacial lake deposits** (Banham Beds)	**Starston Till** / **Glacial sand and gravel**	Mendham Beds (flint-rich sands) / **Starston Till** / Not proved	Beccles 'Glacial' Beds / Mendham Beds / **Starston Till** / Pebbly Series	Corton Formation / Beccles Beds / Kesgrave Formation
pre-Anglian		—	**Kesgrave Sands and Gravels Ingham Sand and Gravel**			
		Chalk	Crag and Chalk	Crag and Chalk	Westleton Beds and Crag	

Lithological units used on the published Diss map are shown bold.

Vertical heavy black bars indicate the range of undifferentiated glacial sand and gravel deposits shown on the published map.

Table 3 Composition of the quartz–quartzite-rich sands and gravels in the +8 to 16 mm size fraction.

	Mineral assessment report areas and height grouping[1]	Number of counts		%flint	%quartz	%quartztite	%others	quartzite: quartz ratio
Ingham Sand and Gravel	Redgrave (area I)	47		46	11	39	4	0.28
	Diss (area II)	2		35	20	44	1	0.45
	Harleston (area III)	10		38	19	40	3	0.48
		59	MEAN	44	13	39	4	0.33
Kesgrave Sands and Gravels	Redgrave (area I)	31		42	16	40	2	0.40
	Diss (area II)	44		40	24	32	4	0.75
	Harleston (area III)	15		57	20	20	3	1.00
		90	MEAN	44	20	33	3	0.61
Alternative classification[1]	Deposits with base >30 m OD	35		41	19	37	3	0.51
	Deposits with base <30 m OD	55		45	22	30	3	0.73
'Reworked Kesgrave Sands and Gravels'	Diss and Harleston (areas II and III)	21		62	18	18	3	1.01

Based largely on data in the Redgrave, Diss and Harleston mineral assessment reports. For areas see Figure 5.

The areas extend beyond the Diss 1:50 000 Sheet.

1 The Kesgrave Sands and Gravels are grouped according to their base levels.

associated with chalky boulder clay, the Lowestoft Till, and which are thought to be of north-western provenance. This classification can be established throughout the district, although in places there is insufficient exposure or other evidence to separate sands and gravels of slightly different composition. Furthermore, although the deposits of north-western provenance generally have a high chalk content (Table 5), this is a poor indicator since chalk pebbles are readily abraded and, if they survive transportation, can be removed by postdepositional solution.

The omnibus informal term Beccles Beds, used on 1:10 000 maps, was introduced (Horton, 1982 a,b; Lawson, 1982) to describe the deposits which are older than those of north-western provenance. It was a term used for a mappable unit that could also be applied to the classification of inadequately described borehole and well records. The base of the Beccles Beds was drawn at the first appearance of large numbers of pebbles. This horizon generally coincides with the top of the Crag, though in some boreholes weathered Crag may have been grouped with the Beccles Beds. The top of the unit was defined by the appearance of deposits rich in chalk which were associated with the Lowestoftian phase of the Anglian glaciation, i.e. the Lowestoft Till, the chalk-flint-rich glacial sand and gravel, etc. Subsequent boreholes showed that the Beccles Beds, as defined, included the Kesgrave Sands and Gravels and the Ingham Sand and Gravel at their base; these generally lie below the modern alluvium. Thus, the greater part of the Beccles Beds outcrop

shown on the 1:10 000 maps consists of sands and gravels of north-eastern origin.

The beds crop out on the steep, grass-covered valley slopes of the River Waveney and are largely obscured by a thin blanket of downwash (head). The few exposures at this stratigraphical level available during 1979–80 indicated a variety of lithological associations within the Beccles Beds. However, given the complex geometry of drift deposits, the lack of exposure and the veneer of Head, it was not possible to subdivide the Beccles Beds outcrop. The subsequent mineral assessment boreholes confirmed the nature of the drift sequence and the diversity of the deposits of north-eastern provenance. These were subdivided, and the term Beccles Beds became less appropriate, being applied to poorly described sequences only.

Kesgrave Sands and Gravels

The term 'Kesgrave Sands and Gravels' was proposed for pale-coloured quartz- and quartzite-rich deposits in Suffolk by Rose et al. (1976). These workers interpreted the Kesgrave Sands and Gravels as braided-river deposits laid down under periglacial conditions during the Beestonian Stage. Palaeocurrent data suggest that the river (or rivers) flowed from the London Basin north-eastwards across East Anglia (Rose and Allen, 1977). The quartz and quartzite pebbles, whose abundance characterises the deposits, are thought to have been derived from outcrops of Sherwood

Sandstone Group ('Bunter Pebble Beds') in the Midlands; rare pebbles of volcanic rocks were probably derived from North Wales (Hey and Brenchley, 1977). The relative contributions of glacial, as opposed to fluvial, processes in transporting these pebbles to East Anglia is difficult to assess. Work by Hey (1980) and Allen (1984) has identified three south-west–north-east aligned tracts of quartz-rich gravel deposits within the Kesgrave Sands and Gravels, each at a different level; it has been suggested that the older, higher-level deposits may be pre-Pastonian in age.

In the south-west of the district, the Kesgrave Sands and Gravels crop out along the flanks of several tributary valleys in the Hinderclay–Redgrave–Wortham area, south of the Waveney–Little Ouse valley (Figure 5). Hereabouts, the Kesgrave Sands and Gravels rest on an undulating surface of the Upper Chalk, generally at elevations between 30 and 40 m above OD. The height of the base of the deposit falls abruptly between Thrandeston [114 765] and Brome [135 765]. East of Brome, the Kesgrave Sands and Gravels rest on Crag at between 20 and 30 m above OD; there, they are generally buried beneath Anglian deposits, except for an outcrop on the south side of the Waveney valley around Oakley [166 780].

Farther north, the deposits are largely cut out by later glacigenic deposits, although the poor quality of many of the borehole records often makes classification difficult. In the south-east, deposits previously classified as Kesgrave Sands and Gravels (Wilcox and Stanczyszyn, 1983; Auton et al., 1985) lie at even lower elevations (base below 15 m above OD). These occurrences are the result of local reworking of 'Kesgrave' type material and are discussed later.

Lithologically, the Kesgrave Sands and Gravels comprise unfossiliferous medium- to coarse-grained sands, with pebbly seams and gravel lenses, and commonly laminated silt and clay, in beds up to 3.0 m thick. The composition of pebbles in the +8 to 16 mm size range, classified on the basis of area and elevation, is shown in Table 4.

The maximum preserved thickness of the Kesgrave Sands and Gravels is 12.2 m in borehole TM07NE [0574 7638], near Redgrave, although they generally range in thickness

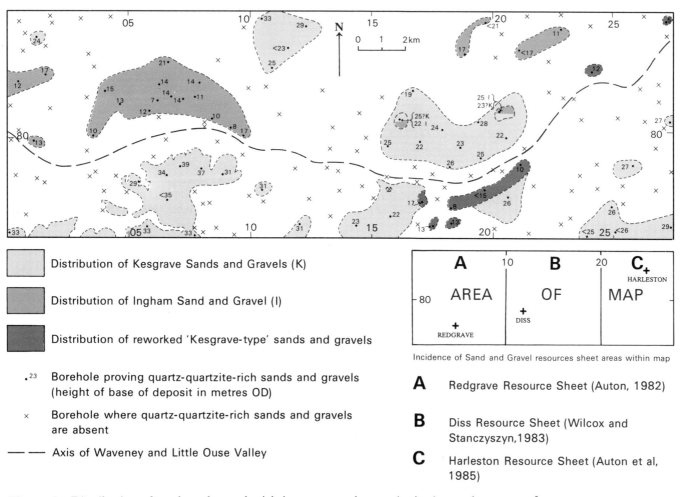

Distribution of Kesgrave Sands and Gravels (K)

Distribution of Ingham Sand and Gravel (I)

Distribution of reworked 'Kesgrave-type' sands and gravels

.23 Borehole proving quartz-quartzite-rich sands and gravels (height of base of deposit in metres OD)

× Borehole where quartz-quartzite-rich sands and gravels are absent

— — Axis of Waveney and Little Ouse Valley

Incidence of Sand and Gravel resources sheet areas within map

A   Redgrave Resource Sheet (Auton, 1982)

B   Diss Resource Sheet (Wilcox and Stanczyszyn, 1983)

C   Harleston Resource Sheet (Auton et al, 1985)

Figure 5   Distribution of sands and gravels rich in quartz and quartzite in the southern part of the district.

between 3 and 8 m. Detailed information is given in Auton (1982), Wilcox and Stanczyszyn (1983) and Auton et al. (1985).

Ingham Sand and Gravel

Other deposits rich in quartz and quartzite pebbles, referred to as the Ingham Sand and Gravel by Lawson (1982), Clarke (1983) and Clarke and Auton (1984), are present in the adjoining Bury St Edmunds (189) district. They are distinguished from the Kesgrave Sands and Gravels by an abundance of liver-coloured quartzite pebbles. These deposits have subsequently been recognised in boreholes in the Redgrave, Diss and Pulham St Mary areas. There is no evidence to show that the Ingham Sand and Gravel crops out in the district.

The main subcrops (Figure 5) lie in the south-west of the district, north of the Little Ouse–Waveney valley (Auton, 1982); isolated occurrences of deposits regarded as Ingham Sand and Gravel have also been reported farther east in the Dickleburgh [168 825]–Starston [235 843] area (Wilcox and Stanczyszyn, 1983; Auton et al., 1985).

The deposits comprise gravels with predominantly medium-grained sand. In contrast to the Kesgrave Sands and Gravels, clay and silt layers are rare. The pebble composition of the + 8 to 16 mm size fraction of the gravels is shown in Table 3; generally, quartz to quartzite ratios for the deposit are just below 0.5, although the deposits are especially rich in quartzite in the Redgrave area, where the ratio averages 0.28.

The maximum recorded thickness of the Ingham Sand and Gravel is 13.2 m in borehole TM08SE/29 [0917 8038], near Roydon, where the base of the deposit lies at an unusually low elevation (8 m above OD), suggesting that the deposit may infill a buried channel. Commonly, the base of the deposit lies between 10 and 17 m above OD, although exceptionally, it may lie at elevations up to 25 m above OD, as in borehole TM28SW/39 [2026 8095]. Over much of its distribution, the deposit is about 5 m thick.

Like the Kesgrave Sands and Gravels, the Ingham Sand and Gravel is thought to comprise braided-river deposits.

Age and origin of the Kesgrave Sands and Gravels and the Ingham Sand and Gravel

Originally, the term Kesgrave Sands and Gravels was applied to most of the quartzite gravels laid down in the present district (Hey, 1980; Allen, 1984). The separation of the Ingham Sand and Gravel from this unit is based on its higher proportion of liver-coloured quartzite pebbles. Although this is an important character, the units are difficult to differentiate, partly because of inherent lateral and vertical variations in lithology within a drift sequence, and partly because the only evidence is from samples from boreholes drilled in the mineral assessment areas.

Both deposits have been tentatively identified in boreholes east of Diss, but their age relationships are contradictory. Thus, Kesgrave Sands and Gravels overlie Ingham Sand and Gravel in borehole TM18SE/43 [1608 8061] near Scole (Wilcox and Stanczyszyn, 1983), but the reverse stratigraphical order has been recorded farther east in borehole

TM28SW/39 [2026 8095] near Thorpe Abbots (Auton et al., 1985).

The Ingham Sand and Gravel and the Kesgrave Sands and Gravels are clearly separable geographically and by a difference in elevation in the south-western part of the district (Figure 5). The much lower elevation of the Ingham Sand and Gravel (Auton, 1982) strongly suggests that its deposits are younger than the Kesgrave Sands and Gravels and that they were deposited from a river or rivers which were probably incised into the latter.

Hey (1980) noted that his Kesgrave Sands and Gravels became enriched in quartzite at the expense of quartz when traced northwards in East Anglia. This observation led him to propose the existence of a tributary river joining the main north-easterly flowing system near Thetford. It seems possible that the Ingham Sand and Gravel was laid down by such a tributary. Hopson and Bridge (1987) suggested that the suite of quartz- and quartzite-rich deposits was laid down by two distinct, east-north-easterly flowing river systems. A more southerly river, a 'proto-Thames', aligned through Great Dunmow, Ipswich and Aldeburgh, deposited Kesgrave Sands and Gravels with a high quartz-to-quartzite ratio. Synchronously, a more northerly river, a 'proto-Waveney', aligned through Bury St Edmunds and Diss to Corton, laid down more quartzite-rich deposits including the Ingham Sand and Gravel.

The absence of obvious gradients on the base of the deposits, and the lack of exposures from which to obtain palaeocurrent directions, makes it difficult to assess the relative merits of the regional drainage models of Hey (1980) and Hopson and Bridge (1987). However, Hey (1980) has obtained northward-directed palaeocurrent directions from the Kesgrave Sands and Gravels both to the north and south of the district.

Hey (1980) regarded the Kesgrave Sands and Gravels in the south-west of the district as part of his pre-Pastonian Westland Green Gravel. The Ingham deposits are thus likely to be younger than the pre-Pastonian and older than the Anglian Stage, and may therefore be Pastonian to Beestonian in age; also, they may be synchronous with the youngest and lowest level (Waldringfield) of the Kesgrave Sands and Gravels in Suffolk.

Reworked 'Kesgrave-type sands and gravels'

Generally, the Kesgrave Sands and Gravels lie at about 20 m above OD in the south-eastern part of the district. However, six boreholes have proved material, which has been classified as Kesgrave Sands and Gravels (Wilcox and Stanczyszyn, 1983; Auton et al., 1985), at a much lower base level. This varies from 17 m above OD [1697 7725] in the west to 5 m above OD [2741 8454] in the north-east (Figure 5). These occurrences lie along the line of the present Waveney Valley. These deposits are less rich in quartzite than the typical Kesgrave Sands and Gravels (Table 4) and may represent Kesgrave Sands and Gravels reworked to a lower level by a proto-Waveney river system; the age of such possible reworking is speculative, but it may be Cromerian. They occur at a lower elevation and must therefore be younger than the Ingham Sand and Gravel. On the 1:50 000 geological map horizontal section, the reworked 'Kesgrave-type Sands and Gravels' is included within the glacial sand and gravel (*sensu lato*).

Other pre-Anglian deposits

A thin layer of red and grey mottled sandy clay resting on Kesgrave Sands and Gravels has been recorded in two boreholes, TM27NW/23 [2383 7592] and TM27NE/6 [2577 7870], in the south-eastern part of the district; these proved 0.8 and 1.4 m of the deposit respectively. The reddened clay layers have been interpreted as palaeosols by Auton et al. (1985) and may be equivalent to the widespread temperate Valley Farm *sol lessivé* described by Rose and Allen (1977) and Kemp (1985). The Valley Farm soil was initially ascribed to the Cromerian (Rose and Allen, 1977), but was later regarded as being more complex, comprising several phases of soil evolution ranging from the Pastonian to Cromerian (Kemp, 1985).

Possible pre-Anglian or early Anglian sediments have been proved in three boreholes in the south-eastern part of the district. A borehole (TM 28NE/25) [2538 8918] near Hospital Farm, Alburgh, proved 18.5 m of Lowestoft Till above 7.7 m of Starston Till, overlying 0.2 m of gravel, rested on 6.1 m of organic silt containing a 1.1 m-thick peat, with thin Crag at the base. The humic sediments contain a diverse insect fauna and pollen, which indicate a cool temperate climate during deposition (Taylor and Coope, 1985). The age of the deposit is uncertain but could be Pastonian or Cromerian.

Borehole TM 28SW/45 [2270 8170], west of Needham, proved 8.8 m of Beccles 'Glacial Beds', on 3.6 m of Starston Till, on 9.9 m of pebbly sand and gravel, which is thought to form part of the Pebbly Series (Auton et al., 1985), resting on Crag. The lowest drift unit contains three fossiliferous humic horizons: a 1.1 m bed of sandy, laminated silt, which immediately underlies the Starston Till, contains beetles and ichneumon flies; a lower 0.1 m-thick bed contains, in addition, mites and fish vertebrae; the lowest horizon, some 13 m above the base, yields beetles only. The fauna indicate that the sediment accumulated under cold continental conditions and may represent an interstadial stage within the early Anglian (Taylor and Coope, 1985).

A borehole (TM 27NE/9) [2672 7769] at The Hall, Fressingfield, proved 13.5 m of Lowestoft Till, on 8.3 m of Starston Till, which rested on 0.2 m of peaty clay and 0.5 m of peat, overlying Westleton Beds.

SEVEN

Quaternary drift—Anglian

All the glacigenic deposits within the district are thought to be Anglian in age *sensu* Shotton and West (1969) and Banham (1971). They comprise the products of two distinct ice sheets, one derived from the north-east which includes the North Sea Drift of Harmer (1909) and, probably, a suite of distinctive glacial lake deposits (the Banham Beds), and the other, from the north-west, which includes the Chalky Boulder Clay (Wood, 1880; Harmer, 1902), now usually referred to as the Lowestoft Till (Baden-Powell, 1948) and its associated outwash deposits.

The north-easterly derived tills and their related outwash sediments include distinctive erratic pebbles of Scandinavian igneous and metamorphic rocks. The Lowestoft Till and its associated outwash deposits are derived from the Mesozoic outcrops to the north-west, principally the Chalk and Kimmeridge Clay.

Field relationships between the two suites of deposits in the Norwich area led Cox and Nickless (1972) to suggest that the two ice sheets were contemporary. The stratigraphical sequence at Corton, near Lowestoft, which is the type section of the Anglian Stage (Banham, 1971), and the work by Bridge and Hopson (1985), indicate, however, that the deposits belong to two distinct phases of the Anglian glaciation. This relationship is supported by the evidence from the Diss district. Representatives of both suites of deposits occur widely, although only the Lowestoft Till has been recognised in the northern parts of the district. The north-easterly derived deposits comprise the Starston Till (Lawson, 1982) and outwash sands and gravels, which correspond to part of the Beccles Beds of Horton (1982a, b) and Auton et al. (1985). The overlying deposits comprise an extensive sheet of till (Lowestoft Till) and waterlaid sediments (glacial sand and gravel, and glacial silt and clay). These later deposits blanket much of the landscape around Diss; exposures of the earlier Anglian Drift are restricted to the sides of valleys incised through the Lowestoft deposits in the south-east of the district.

DRIFT OF NORTH-EASTERN PROVENANCE

Glacial sand and gravel

The glacial sand and gravel (*sensu lato*) depicted on the 1:50 000 map includes deposits of both north-eastern and north-western provenance, broadly characterised by low and medium to high chalk pebble contents respectively. The high solubility of chalk and lack of exposure caused difficulty in distinguishing these units during the field survey. Similar problems faced the geologists undertaking the mineral assessment programme, and the deposits of north-eastern and north-western provenances were only classified as such in the final report covering the south-east and eastern part of the district (Auton et al., 1985). The detailed sequence established there can now only be partly recognised in the boreholes described in the earlier reports (Auton, 1982; Wilcox and Stanczyszyn, 1983). Analyses of the pebble-count data for samples from those boreholes provide evidence for the presence of both types of glacial sand and gravel. The classifications in Table 4 are based both on chalk content and the stratigraphical sequence in the borehole sampled. The sediments thought to be of north-eastern origin have a low chalk pebble content (0–9.9 per cent); in fact most samples are chalk free. The crude results show that glacial sand and gravel of north-western provenance has a much higher chalk content. It therefore seems that a significant proportion of borehole samples in the Diss and Palgrave areas, attributed to this source on lithostratigraphical grounds, but containing few chalk pebbles, are probably of north-eastern origin.

The surveyors (1979–80) of the southern and eastern parts of the district (National Grid sheets 17 NW, NE; 18 all parts; 27 NW, NE; 28 all parts; 29 SW, SE) show the glacial sand and gravel of north-western origin is shown on the 1:10 000 maps. The glacial sand and gravel of north-eastern origin is depicted as Beccles Beds, though in places it is poss-

Table 4 Percentage chalk pebble content of sands and gravels in the +8 to 16 mm grade for glacial sand and gravel of north-western and north-eastern provenance. Samples grouped by lithological and lithostratigraphical units, and by present distribution.	Mineral assessment report	North-western provenance		North-eastern provenance		Total no. of borehole samples
		Percentage chalk content		Percentage chalk content		
		0 to 10%	>10%	0 to 10%	>10%	
	Redgrave (area I)	11	15	15	0	41
	Diss (area II)	11	16	11	0	38	101
	Harleston (area III)	8	0	10	4	22
	Mean	10	12	12	1	

ible that small outcrops of Kesgrave Sands and Gravels may be incorporated. On the 1:50 000 map, the two suites of glacial sand and gravel deposits are undifferentiated.

During the field survey, two distinct lithological members were recognised within the Beccles Beds outcrop, the Mendham Beds (mostly glacial sand and gravel of north-eastern provenance) and the Starston Till. The BGS mineral assessment drilling programme confirmed the presence of these members and, on the basis of pebble counts, defined additional members which are known only from boreholes (Auton et al., 1985). The upward sequence demonstrated is: Pebbly Series, Starston Till, Mendham Beds and Beccles 'Glacial' Beds. The boreholes showed that thin clays and silts occur throughout these rudaceous and arenacous units, but only one bed, the Starston Till, is of regional significance. The Starston Till generally separates the Pebbly Series from the overlying units of the Beccles Beds. However, beds of similar lithology can occur within the upper part of the Pebbly Series in adjacent areas, and within the overlying Mendham Beds and the Beccles 'Glacial' Beds, thus reflecting the complex interaction of processes at the time of deposition (Auton et al., 1985, p.6) These deposits can be recognised consistently within the south-eastern part of the district, the area assessed for sand and gravel, but elsewhere the borehole records mention only 'sand' and 'gravel' which cannot be classified.

In the Redgrave area, the greater part of the glacial sand and gravel appears to postdate the Lowestoft Till. It includes beds with both very low and high chalk pebble content. Locally, as for example in a borehole [0925 7670], a pebbly sand, which appears to be relatively chalk free, underlies the till and probably equates in part with the glacial sand and gravel of north-eastern provenance, the Beccles Beds.

In the north-western part of the district, glacial sand and gravel of north-eastern origin are included in the unit depicted as glacial lake deposits (Banham Beds on 1:10 000 maps). Deposits of north-western provenance are shown as glacial sand and gravel.

The thickness and distribution of the glacial sand and gravel has been modified extensively by erosion associated with the Lowestoft phase, and their thickness is therefore very variable. The thickest recorded sequence is 22.3 m in borehole TM28SE/25 [2527 8461], but the deposits commonly range from 10 to 20 m thick.

Pebbly Series

This unit formerly embraced all sands and gravels younger than the shelly Crag and older than the Norwich Brickearth (e.g. Whitaker and Dalton, 1887); the latter is probably equivalent to the Starston Till. The term is here restricted to that part of the former Pebbly Series which succeeds the Westleton Beds, Kesgrave Sands and Gravels and Ingham Sand and Gravel. It is overlain by the Starston Till, the Mendham Beds or the Beccles 'Glacial' Beds. The Pebbly Series so defined comprises pebbly sands and sandy gravels similar in composition to the underlying units. However, the gravel is generally coarser, the flint pebbles more angular and the proportion of quartz and quartzite slightly lower. Chalk is also present locally, but igneous and metamorphic pebbles are rare.

The Pebbly Series has been proved in six boreholes in the Weybread–Harleston area, in the east of the district; these proved upwards of 6.3 m of beds. The complete sequence was proved in one borehole [2454 8076], where 14.7 m of beds resting on ?Westleton Beds are overlain by Lowestoft Till. The greatest, but incomplete thickness was proved in a borehole TM28SE/26 [2527 8461] north-east of Harleston, where Beccles 'Glacial Beds' overlie 18.3 m of pebbly sand and sandy gravel.

Mendham Beds

The Mendham Beds overlie the Pebbly Series and, in places, lie both above and below, and locally interbedded with the Starston Till; the type section is Mendham Pit [2716 8245]. They comprise fine- to medium-grained quartz sands with rare seams of, and scattered subangular flints. They are restricted to the eastern edge of the district around Harleston. At the type site, they are 11 m thick, and in the three boreholes in which they have been recorded the thickness ranges from 8.0 m [2596 8356] to 9.3 m [2318 7663]. Lawson (1982) interpreted the deposits as distal fluvioglacial sediments.

Beccles 'Glacial' Beds

The Beccles 'Glacial' Beds are known only from boreholes and have been proved to the east of a line from Chickering to Darrow Green, in the eastern and south-eastern parts of the district. They generally constitute the youngest sand and gravel member of the Beccles Beds and are in places overlain by the drift deposits of north-western provenance. Elsewhere, the Beccles 'Glacial' Beds are succeeded by diamictons correlated with the Starston Till, but similar lithologies occur both interbedded with and beneath this member. The Beccles 'Glacial' beds are undoubtedly younger than the Pebbly Series.

The Beccles 'Glacial' Beds consist of pebbly sands, the fine gravel fraction of which consists primarily of angular flint clasts with subordinate flint, quartz and quartzite pebbles. Locally, chalk pebbles, coarse angular chalk sand grains and thin beds of laminated silt and clay occur.

The thickest developments were recorded in boreholes near Syleham [2209 7852] and Weybread [2474 7992], both of which failed to reach the base and which proved 17.4 and 11.4 m respectively.

Starston Till

The term Starston Till was proposed by Lawson (1982) for a sandy till with a small proportion of igneous and metamorphic erratics which are thought to be of Scandanavian origin. As defined, it formed a member within the Beccles Beds. The till was initially recognised by Whitaker and Dalton (1887) who referred to it as Lower Boulder Clay. Lawson (1982) regarded the Starston Till as a correlative of the Norwich Brickearth, a part of the Drift of north-eastern provenance, which is present in the Norwich area, to the north-east of the present district. Lithologically, it resembles the Cromer Tills, exposed in cliff sections in north Norfolk.

The Starston Till crops out locally only near Starston village [235 843]. There, it comprises a sandy silty clay with sporadic pebbles, including scattered small chalk pebbles, and angular flints. Generally, the deposit is massive, though lamination was noted by Lawson.

The most easily recognised feature of the Starston Till is its brown colour. This is generally olive-brown to brownish grey, but it ranges from orange-brown to yellow-brown to dusky brown. The deposit is commonly a silty and sandy clay with sporadic small pebbles. The grain size distribution of the matrix (Figure 6; Bloodworth, 1986) is clearly distinct from that of the diamictons (?tills) in the glacial lake deposits, which crop out in the north-west of the district, and of the Lowestoft Till. Fine gravel (+ 4 to − 8mm) analyses of the enclosed pebbles also show a marked contrast (Figure 8b). Locally, the Starston Till contains up to 50 per cent of chalk pebbles (by weight), although chalk is generally less abundant and averages 22.6 per cent of the pebble content. Chalk also occurs as coarse-grained sand. The minor pebble components include granitoids, porphyritic and nonporphyritic lavas, and schists: they are absent from the other suites of glacial deposits in the district. Marine shells and shell debris, which have also been recorded from the Starston Till, are probably derived from the Crag. Some of the boreholes show interbedded sands and even gravel seams; in others two seams of Starston Till lithology can be present.

Lithologies comparable to the Starston Till were recognised in the BGS mineral assessment boreholes throughout the southern half of the district. They occur at a variety of horizons, and the use of the term Starston Till for these deposits is a major extension of its original definition. Deposits of Starston Till lithology most commonly occur immediately beneath the sequence of drift deposits of north-western provenance and particularly the Lowestoft Till (Table 5). In at least a third of the boreholes, the Starston Till occurs either within the Beccles 'Glacial' Beds or, more commonly, between them and the underlying members of the Beccles Beds, i.e. the Mendham Beds and the Pebbly Series. It probably occurs at this horizon in the type area. It may also occur between the drift deposits of north-eastern provenance and the Westleton Beds or the Crag.

The Starston Till has not been recognised at outcrop beyond its type area. It forms a discontinuous sheet across the southern part of the district (Figure 7). It may crop out locally at the base of the Lowestoft Till, but is difficult to recognise in the absence of sections and has not been confirmed by mapping. In the northern part of the district, where there are no BGS boreholes through the drift sequence, the Starston Till may have been cut out by the succeeding Lowestoft Till. However, small concealed remnants remain, such as that recorded in Morningthorpe Gravel Pit [2206 9455], where a channel fill of Starston Till cuts into the Crag deposits (Wyatt, 1981).

At present the most westerly known occurrence within the Diss Sheet is in a borehole [0038 7846] west of Thelnetham, where 7.8 m of Starston Till underlie Lowestoft Till. The maximum thickness of the Starston Till was recorded in a borehole [2147 8046] west of Newditch Farm, Brockdish, where 1.4 m of yellowish brown sandy clay with pebbles of chalk, quartz, quartzite and flint overlay 0.8 m of sand and a further 7.6 m of sandy clay without reaching the base. The till was proved in 49 of the mineral assessment boreholes drilled over the southern part of the sheet; in half of these, the thickness lay between 1 and 3 m (Table 6).

As originally defined, the Starston Till is interbedded with the fluvioglacial deposits of the Beccles Beds. Although

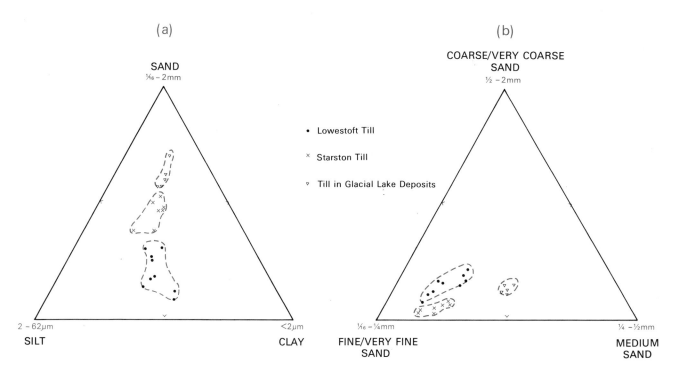

Figure 6   Triangular plots of the matrix grain-size distribution for Anglian tills.

Table 5   Number of boreholes penetrating stratigraphical horizons in which the Starston Till occurs in the southern and south-eastern parts of the district.

Stratigraphical horizon		Number of boreholes								Percentage	
		Redgrave (area A)		Diss (area B)		Harleston (area C)		Total number of boreholes			
	Below Lowestoft Till	4		10		9		23		41	
Deposits of north-western provenance	Below Glacial sand and gravel	8	12	–	10	1	11	9	33	16	59
	Below channel fill deposits	–		–		1		1		2	
Deposits of north-eastern provenance	Within Beccles 'Glacial' Beds	3		–		3		6		11	
	Below Beccles 'Glacial' Beds	2	7	3	4	7	12	12	23	21	41
	In Pebbly Series	–		–		2		2		4	
	Below ?Beccles 'Glacial' Beds or ?Glacial sand and gravel	2		1		–		3		5	

The area of the mineral assessment report is shown in Figure 5.

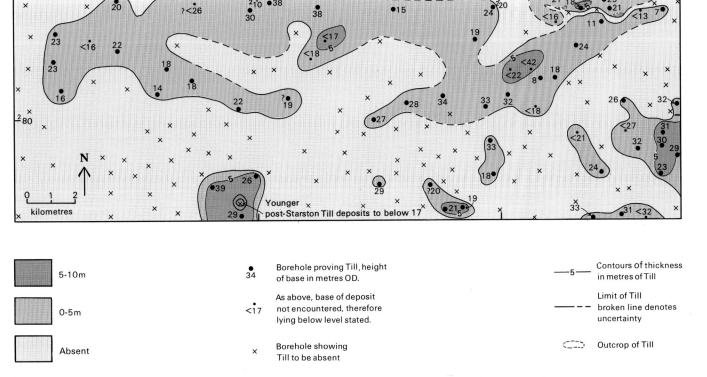

■ 5-10m	● 34 Borehole proving Till, height of base in metres OD.	—5— Contours of thickness in metres of Till
▨ 0-5m	<17 As above, base of deposit not encountered, therefore lying below level stated.	- - - Limit of Till, broken line denotes uncertainty
□ Absent	× Borehole showing Till to be absent	⬭ Outcrop of Till

Figure 7   Distribution, height of base and thickness of the Starston Till in the southern part of the district.

Table 6   Thickness distribution of the Starston Till in boreholes in the southern and south-eastern parts of the district.

Mineral assessment report areas	Thickness in metres									
	0–1	1–2	2–3	3–4	4–5	5–6	6–7	7–8	8–9	>9
Redgrave (area I)	5	4	6	1	–	2	–	1	1	
Diss (area II)	3	4	1	2	–	–	–	–	1	1
Harleston (area III)	1	5	4	1	1	2	1	–	1	1
Total number of boreholes	9	13	11	4	1	4	1	1	3	2

Mineral assessment report areas as in Figure 5.

described as a till, there are indications that it was in part water-laid. The new sections confirm the presence of interbedded seams of sand and also fine gravel. Harmer (1902) considered that its lateral equivalent, the Norwich Brickearth, may have been deposited in a proglacial lake environment. In contrast, it has been suggested that the Norwich Brickearth was deposited directly from an ice sheet as a structureless lodgement till (Cox et al., 1989). In the Redgrave area, the Starston Till (then known as the brown sandy basal till) forms a sheet draping the undulating surface of the older drift deposits and solid rocks, a distribution more typical of a lodgement till than of a quiet-water sediment. The deposit probably formed in part by all these processes and also locally as a flow till (Horton, 1982b).

Glacial lake deposits

The glacial lake deposits are confined to the north-west of the district, in the Banham [065 882] and East Harling [TL 994 886] areas, and have been termed 'Banham Beds' by

Plate 1   Well-sorted, medium-grained, cross-bedded sand of the Mendham Beds, overlain by laminated, water-laid, stony, sandy clay of the Starston Till. The upper part of the till is the weathered soil horizon. Road cutting north of Wortwell [2738 8542]. (A 13982)

Mathers et al. (1987). The deposits lie beneath the Lowestoft Till, from which they can be distinguished readily by their abundant quartz and quartzite pebble content (Figure 8) and their general lack of chalk.

The deposits crop out along the valley sides in the Banham–Kenninghall–East Harling area (Mathers, 1988; Zalasiewicz, 1988). They rest, at between 30 and 40 m above OD, on the fairly even surface of the Chalk which slopes gently to the south-east (Figure 9). Mapping suggests that, in detail, the Chalk surface is irregular. The deposits are generally from 4 to 8 m thick, although thicker sequences may be preserved in hollows cut into the Chalk. The present outcrops are remnants of a much more extensive deposit which was eroded by later glacial processes.

The glacial lake deposits comprise a lithologically variable sequence of silts and clays, with subordinate diamicts, sands and gravels. This variability has made it impracticable to map individual lithologies within the sequence. The silts and clays are poorly to well laminated and contain isolated pebbles of quartz and quartzite, and angular black flints with a maximum size of 40 mm; these are probably dropstones. Locally, thin laminae of fine- to medium-grained sand are also present, together with seams of pebbles. The diamicts comprise a pale grey, stiff sandy clay in which sporadic granules and pebbles of quartz and quartzite, and angular flint are embedded. The diamicts are up to 3 m thick and strongly overconsolidated, and are regarded as tills, although similar beds elsewhere have been interpreted as water-laid sediments (Horton, 1970, p.4). Lenses of sand and gravel are common within the glacial lake deposits, especially at the base of a sequence. The pebble composition of the glacial lake deposits is distinct from that of the Kesgrave and Ingham sand and gravel deposits (Figure 8A) and also from the Starston and Lowestoft tills (Figure 8B). Typical sequences of glacial lake deposits are illustrated in Figure 9.

The variability of the sequences suggests changing depositional environments, perhaps indicative of an ice-marginal regime. The absence of Scandinavian indicator pebbles makes it difficult to assign these deposits to the earlier, north-easterly derived phase with certainty, and on present evidence a pre-Anglian age for them cannot be ruled out. Provisionally, however, these deposits are grouped with the Anglian Drift of north-eastern provenance.

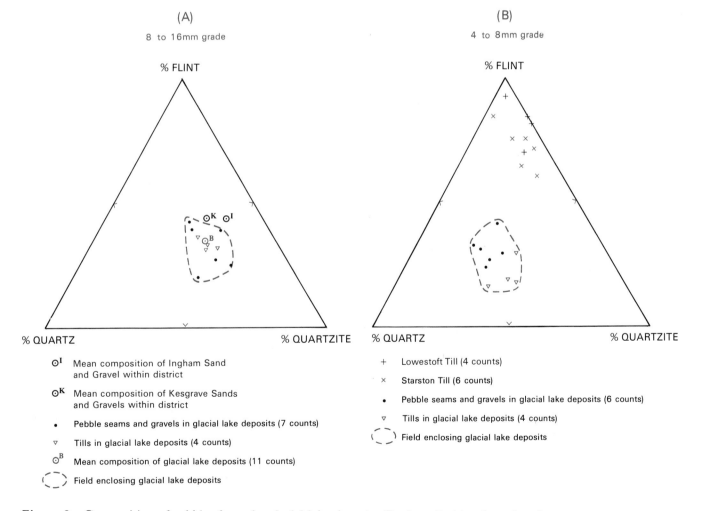

Figure 8 Composition of pebbles from the glacial lake deposits (Banham Beds); triangular plots of percentages of flint, quartz and quartzite.

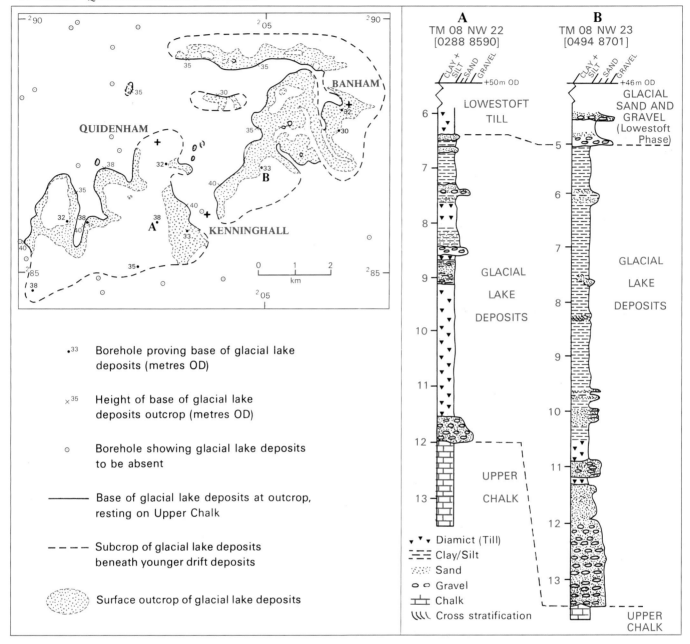

Figure 9 Distribution and lithological sequences of the glacial lake deposits (Banham Beds) around Kenninghall.

DRIFT OF NORTH-WESTERN PROVENANCE

These deposits comprise glacial silt and clay, the Lowestoft Till and the younger glacial sand and gravel unit. Together, they form an extensive sheet from 20 to 30 m in thickness, although locally it may exceed 50 m, and cover about 80 per cent of the surface in the district. However, within buried channels, sequences as much as 75 m thick are preserved containing varied successions comprising all three of the above lithologies. The most important member is the Lowestoft Till, the outcrop of which gives rise to the extensive upland which constitutes much of the Diss Sheet.

Buried channels are developed along the Waveney–Little Ouse valley, and beneath some of their tributaries; other buried channels are known beneath Attleborough and the Tas valley (see inset diagram on 1:50 000 map). Sporadic boreholes which prove anomalously thick Drift sequences suggest the occurrence of further channels. The channels may be incised through older Drift into Chalk or, in the south-east of the district, into Crag. Woodland (1970) has shown that, in East Anglia, some of these channels may have undulating thalwegs and be closed at their downstream ends. He interpreted them as subglacial meltwater channels in which water confined by the overlying ice sheet could erode the bedrock, commonly under considerable hydrostatic pressure. However, it has been suggested (Cox, 1985) that at least some of the channels, including that beneath the Tas Valley near Norwich, are pre-Anglian river valleys that have been modified by glacial processes. Deep buried channels in the Hamburg area, Germany, are thought to have resulted from the catastrophic release of englacial or subglacial meltwater in the marginal parts of an ice sheet (Ehlers and Linke, 1989). When the water velocity decreased, the channels were filled with glacier ice, which may have restricted the channels. When the ice retreated, a mixture of meltwater and proglacial lake sediments infilled the depressions.

Glacial silt and clay

The glacial silt and clay, which is shown as glacial laminated deposits on the 1:10 000 maps, comprises both massive, indefinitely bedded sediments, usually silt, and regularly laminated silts and clays with thin partings and interbeds of fine- and very fine-grained sand. Thin seams of chalk and flint pebbles are also present locally. It is generally pale olive-grey when fresh, but weathers to a yellowish brown colour.

Small outcrops occur throughout the district; most are associated with the modern valleys. Thin seams can occur within the Lowestoft Till or within the glacial sand and gravel, but the thicker developments occur interbedded with these lithologies, commonly infilling deep drift-filled buried channels (channel-fill deposits). The glacial silt and clay are glacigenic deposits laid down in bodies of standing water. They are considered by some workers to have been deposited in tunnel valleys beneath the ice sheet, but are thought by others to have been deposited in proglacial lakes. The intricate sequences along the margins of the Waveney buried channel reflect a complex history of infilling.

The glacial silt and clay lithologies, particularly where forming part of the channel-fill deposits, appear to be closely comparable with those of the older glacial lake deposits (p.22). Both suites may have been deposited in a proglacial environment, the latter in association with an ice sheet, possibly earlier than, but probably contemporaneous with that which laid down the drifts of north-eastern provenance, and the former with the main Anglian Lowestoft-phase ice sheet.

Details

Within the Thet drainage basin, several small outcrops of glacial silt and clay are present near Banham [064 882], East Harling Common [002 879] and North End [001 923]. The deposits comprise up to 4 m of grey, massive and laminated silts and clays.

In the north-east, around Hempnall [242 944], there are several outcrops of glacial silt and clay around the head of one of the tributary valleys of the River Tas. Farther west, a similar deposit is exposed in a gravel pit [217 944] north of Morningthorpe (Wyatt, 1981). There, some 3.8 m of laminated silts and clays, which are very sandy near their base, occur beneath Lowestoft Till and overlie glacial sand and gravel. These deposits were probably laid down in a proglacial lake (Wyatt, 1981) and subsequently overridden by ice.

Glacial silt and clay is extensive within the buried channel along the Waveney valley. Laminated silts and clays are exposed on the valley sides, for example to the west of Palgrave [100 790] and west of Scole [140 793]. Thick sequences have been proved beneath the floodplain of the River Waveney, for example in borehole TM07NE/23 [0542 7959] where over 17.1 m are present, and in

borehole TM08SE/18 [0583 8049] where an unbottomed sequence of 16.6 m was encountered.

Lowestoft Till

An extensive sheet of Lowestoft Till blankets much of the Diss district. It has a fairly flat upper surface which produces the broad plateau landscape characteristic of much of East Anglia. The Chalky Boulder Clay of East Anglia (Wood, 1880; Harmer, 1902) was initally envisaged as a single lithological unit. However, Boswell (1931) subdivided it into two units, which were subsequently defined by Baden-Powell (1948, 1950) and West and Donner (1956) as the Lowestoft Till below and Gipping Till above (Wolstonian), supposedly separated by the Hoxnian interglacial. Subsequent field investigations (Bristow and Cox, 1973; Cox, 1981) and detailed mineralogical and grain size analyses (Perrin et al., 1973, 1979) favour the concept of a single chalky till unit. Some support for the existence of two tills was expressed by Straw (1979), who regarded the chalky boulder clay in the western part of the district as Wolstonian in age. The recent field survey found no topographical demarcation or lithological distinction between his till units (Horton, 1982a, b). In practice, distinguishing between superimposed sheets of chalky till is extremely difficult, unless intervening interglacial deposits or weathered horizons can be demonstrated. No such intervening deposits are known within the district, but Hoxnian interglacial deposits overlie the Lowestoft Till (see below).

Boreholes indicate that the Lowestoft Till is very variable in thickness. In central northern parts of the district, between Old Buckenham [067 915] and Bunwell [125 928], over 50 m have been recorded from several boreholes. Elsewhere, the deposit is commonly between 10 and 30 m thick, except where it occupies buried channels or depressions. One example is borehole TM09SW/16 [0010 9229], near Snetterton, where some 52.4 m of till are present. Within the Lowestoft Till, there are lenses of laminated silts and clays, and stratified sands and gravels, but individually these rarely exceed 2.0 m in thickness, except close to some buried channels where till interdigitates with much thicker sequences of water-laid deposits.

The Lowestoft Till is a matrix-supported diamict. Near surface the deposit is usually oxidised to a yellow-brown colour and is decalcified. The unweathered matrix comprises greyish black silty clay probably made of reconstituted Kimmeridge Clay and other Mesozoic argillaceous rocks. Numerous clasts up to boulder size are embedded within this matrix. Clasts of rounded chalk commonly less than 40 mm in diameter are dominant, and flint, which ranges in size from small flakes to entire nodules, is also common. Minor components include silicified limestone, shell material, mudstone and sandstone derived from Mesozoic rocks, quartz and quartzite pebbles, and fragments of iron pan derived from the Kesgrave Sands and Gravels and the Crag.

The provenance of the constituent materials, coupled with measurements of the included pebble fabrics (West and Donner, 1956) and regional trends within the composition of the matrix (Perrin et al., 1979), suggest that the Lowestoft Till was laid down by ice flowing eastwards or south-eastwards across the district.

Most of the Lowestoft Till is probably a lodgement till, although other processes of till formation, including deformation and flowage, are likely to have contributed in part.

Glacial sand and gravel

The outwash sands and gravels from the Lowestoft phase of glaciation constitute the younger component of the glacial sand and gravel shown on the 1:50 000 map. In general, they are coarser, much more poorly sorted and more variable than the outwash deposits of the early Anglian Drift (of north-eastern provenance) which are also included in the omnibus glacial sand and gravel unit. The younger glacial sand and gravel deposits are probably equivalent to similar deposits in Suffolk, which have been termed Barham Sands and Gravels by Rose and Allen (1977).

The Lowestoft-phase deposits range from flint- and chalk-rich cobble gravels, with cobbles in excess of 30 cm across, to fine-grained sands, and are variably clayey. The principal gravel-size clasts are of angular and nodular flint, which commonly make up over half the gravel fraction by weight. The chalk pebble content is very variable (0 to 72 per cent) due, in part, to differential decalcification. Minor components commonly include quartz, quartzite, limestone, sandstone and dolerite pebbles, and Mesozoic shell fragments. Bearing in mind the effect of any decalcification, the gravel fraction reflects that of the resistant clasts in the associated Lowestoft Till. Commonly the sand component is mainly quartz, with subordinate flint and chalk. The Lowestoft-phase glacial sand and gravel occurs within buried channels and as beds beneath, within and above the main Lowestoft Till sheet.

Thickest developments commonly occur in channel fill deposits, for example in the buried channel beneath the Waveney valley, where sequences of glacial sand and gravel are commonly over 20 m thick; the deposits comprise gravel and pebbly sands, some of which are clayey. Farther north, near Attleborough Station, borehole TM09SE/12 [0514 9493] proved 21.9 m of glacial sand and gravel occupying the bottom of part of a channel system.

A fairly continuous sheet of glacial sand and gravel is depicted on the 1:50 000 map beneath the Lowestoft Till in the south-west, central and north-western parts of the district. The deposits are generally up to 20 m thick and probably locally include beds equivalent to the Beccles

Figure 10 Selected sequences of glacial sand and gravel at the Snetterton Heath and Beacon Hill pits.

'Glacial' Beds. In the north-west, the poor quality of the borehole records makes it impossible to distinguish these deposits from the early Anglian outwash sands and gravels. The sheet of glacial sand and gravel at the base of the Lowestoft Till probably represents proximal proglacial outwash that was subsequently overridden by the advancing ice sheet.

Beyond the limits of the buried channels, boreholes indicate that impersistent lenticular bodies, up to 5 m thick, of glacial sand and gravel occur locally within the Lowestoft Till. The origin of these deposits is uncertain. Some may be englacial, whilst others could perhaps represent local short-lived retreat phases.

Small spreads of glacial sand and gravel overlying, or demonstrably postdating the regional Lowestoft Till are common. By far the most extensive are in the north-western quadrant of the district, where the deposits have cut through the till to rest on glacial lake deposits or on Chalk. Such deposits are exposed in a pit [013 900] at Gallows Hill, Snetterton Heath. Several patches are also present adjacent to the Waveney valley (Bristow, 1986). Data from boreholes and mapping show that such occurrences are of very variable thickness. In some areas, they comprise a sheet up to 2 m thick, whereas elsewhere, they may thicken to 10 m thick in channels, and may include thin silt, clay and till layers.

Graphic logs of selected sections and gravel composition analyses are given in Figure 10. The deposits in the Snetterton Heath pit are disturbed by high-angle normal and reverse faults, suggesting that they may have been laid down on top of, or in contact with ice. Coxon (1979, 1984) reached a similar conclusion about glacial sand and gravel deposits at Roydon Pit [099 802] in the Waveney valley, which he termed High Level Gravel. The spreads of glacial sand and gravel which overlie the Lowestoft Till sheet represent the final depositional event of the Lowestoft phase of glaciation. As such, they represent ice-marginal outwash deposits, perhaps produced around a stationary or stagnating ice front. Their distribution suggests that both the Waveney valley and a proto-Thet drainage system were important pathways for meltwaters at the close of the Anglian Stage.

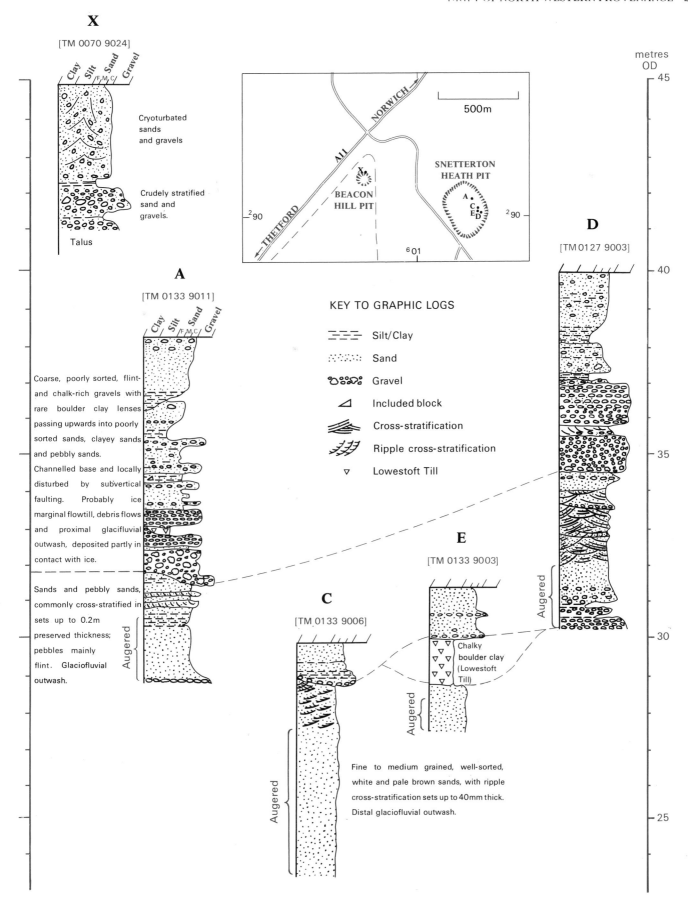

X

[TM 0070 9024]

Clay · Silt · Sand (F, M, C) · Gravel

Cryoturbated sands and gravels

Crudely stratified sand and gravels.

Talus

A

[TM 0133 9011]

Clay · Silt · Sand (F, M, C) · Gravel

Coarse, poorly sorted, flint- and chalk-rich gravels with rare boulder clay lenses passing upwards into poorly sorted sands, clayey sands and pebbly sands. Channelled base and locally disturbed by subvertical faulting. Probably ice marginal flowtill, debris flows and proximal glacifluvial outwash, deposited partly in contact with ice.

Sands and pebbly sands, commonly cross-stratified in sets up to 0.2m preserved thickness; pebbles mainly flint. Glaciofluvial outwash.

Augered

500m

NORWICH

THETFORD

A11

BEACON HILL PIT

SNETTERTON HEATH PIT

A
C
E
D

²90

²90

⁶01

KEY TO GRAPHIC LOGS

Silt/Clay

Sand

Gravel

Included block

Cross-stratification

Ripple cross-stratification

Lowestoft Till

D

[TM 0127 9003]

Augered

E

[TM 0133 9003]

Chalky boulder clay (Lowestoft Till)

Augered

C

[TM 0133 9006]

Augered

Fine to medium grained, well-sorted, white and pale brown sands, with ripple cross-stratification sets up to 40mm thick. Distal glaciofluvial outwash.

metres OD

45

40

35

30

25

EIGHT

Quaternary drift—Hoxnian to Flandrian

Interglacial silt and clay

Interglacial silt and clay deposits around Hoxne [175 767] include the type sequence for the temperate Hoxnian Stage of the Pleistocene (West, 1956; Mitchell et al., 1973). Prior to their almost complete removal as material for brick-making, these deposits, the Hoxne Beds, occupied an elongate former lake basin, some 570 m long and up to 14 m deep, cut within the regional sheet of Lowestoft Till on a north-east-pointing spur overlooking the valley of the River Dove (Figure 11).

The depression has been interpreted as a kettle hole left after the wastage of the Anglian ice (West, 1956). The sediments that infill the basin consist of up to 7 m of uniform, calcareous silty clays. These are sandwiched be-tween a thin, variable basal bed with pebbly layers and scattered plant debris, and an uppermost thin, finer-grained, peaty, noncalcareous clay, overlain by post-Hoxnian sands, silts and gravels, laid down in cooler climatic conditions (Plate 2).

This lacustrine sequence contains pollen which show the progression from a Late-glacial cool climate through warm Early-temperate and Late-temperate climates (Figure 11; West, 1956). This amelioration is marked by an expansion of woodland; at first birch (pollen substage I) and then pine (substage IIa), oak (substage IIb), alder (substage IIc), and finally elm and alder (substage IId). A decline in trees and an increase in grasses near the top of substage IId has been interpreted as being due to either a widespread forest fire

Plate 2   Head gravel, comprising crudely bedded sand and gravelly sand overlying poorly sorted gravel, resting on laminated silt and clay of the Hoxne Beds, Hoxne [175 767]. (A 11433)

Figure 11 Interglacial silt and clay deposits (Hoxne Beds) at Hoxne; stratigraphy, lithology and pollen analysis.

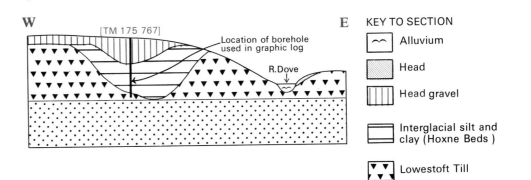

(West, 1956) or a slight climatic fluctuation (Wymer, 1983). The peaty, noncalcareous lake clays at the top of the lacustrine sequence contain pollen indicating the Late-temperate Hoxnian (substage III), with a decline in oak and elm; they have been interpreted in terms of a fall of water table around the lake.

An erosional hiatus marks the top of the Hoxnian sequence, and there is little evidence of the post-temperate part of the Hoxnian Stage, subsequently recognised in the more complete sequence at Marks Tey, in Essex (Turner, 1970).

A borehole at Frenze Hall, Scole (TM 18SW/57) [1333 8038] proved 5.3 m of pebbly sand, possibly glacial sand and gravel, resting on 6.7 m of humic silt, above chalky till. The age of the silt is uncertain, other than being post-Anglian.

Head deposits

Head deposits are produced by processes such as solifluxion, hillwash and soil creep, which move materials downslope into valleys and depressions. The resulting deposits are commonly closely associated with fluvial sediments. Extensive head deposits are more likely to have developed during cold climatic conditions, when reduced vegetation cover, increased precipitation and run off, together with cryoturbation, tended to enhance the downslope transport of materials. Within the district, two types of deposit have been recognised, namely head gravel and head.

HEAD GRAVEL

The distribution of head gravel is very localised; it forms several small remnant patches, mostly resting on Lowestoft Till, in the Oakley–Hoxne and Weybread–Mendham areas.

The deposits comprise clayey, pebbly sand and gravel with thin beds of silt and clay. They are commonly poorly sorted and contain flint and, rarely, chalk pebbles. Locally, the deposits have been cryoturbated together with the underlying till to produce a mixed deposit. Within the district, the head gravels are generally 2 to 3 m thick. Exceptionally, a complex sequence of over 7 m of sands, gravels and silts is preserved overlying the interglacial silt and clay deposits at Hoxne (Plate 2; Wymer, 1974, 1983; Gladfelter, 1975; Horton, 1982a).

Pollen recovered from the lower part of the head gravel at Hoxne is largely derived from the interglacial deposits (West, 1956), but the wood and leaf fragments indicate a cool climate with sparse vegetation that includes dwarf willow and birch. These sediments have yielded important archaeological material, namely numerous flint implements of Acheulian age, together with butchered animal material (Wymer, 1983). The succeeding beds show signs of a slight climatic amelioration (Wymer, 1983), followed by cold climatic conditions which allowed the growth of ice-wedge casts within the sediments and resulted in the brecciation of the clay layers (Figure 11).

The upper part of the head gravel at Hoxne contains poorly sorted clayey sands with gravelly lenses. These were interpreted as deposits of the 'Gipping' (Wolstonian) glaciation (West, 1956). The 'Gipping' glaciation concept has since been discredited (Bristow and Cox, 1973) and the deposits are now interpreted as having been formed by solifluxion and fluvial processes in a periglacial climate (Wymer, 1983).

The head gravels do not occur in present-day topographical depressions; they probably formed as part of an extensive veneer of deposits associated with a proto-Waveney drainage system and have been referred to the Wolstonian Stage (Wymer, 1983).

HEAD

Head deposits, up to 2 m thick, occur widely within the valleys of the district. In the major valleys, they flank the fluvial sediments which form the valley floors, whilst in the smaller tributary valleys, head extends across the valley floors. Since head deposits can become gradually reworked into fluvial deposits by stream action, the sediments often appear transitional in character and their boundaries are somewhat arbitrary. In general, the upslope limit of head is marked by a steepening of the valley slope.

The lithology of the head deposits is controlled by the upslope sediment source. Commonly, several source lithologies contribute, giving rise to very variable poorly sorted

deposits. Within the district, the head mostly comprises soft, poorly sorted, brown clayey sand with scattered angular flints and quartz and quartzite pebbles. Lithological variants include sandy clays and sandy pebbly clays. The deposits are generally chalk free. Unlike the head gravel, the head deposits are closely related to the present-day drainage; they are probably mainly Devensian in age.

River terrace deposits

River terrace deposits are preserved within the drainage systems of the Little Ouse, Waveney, Tas and Thet. Four terrace levels can be recognised in the Little Ouse–Waveney system, which drains the southern half of the district. In the north-west, the River Thet and its tributaries possess two main terraces. In the north-east, only one small patch of river terrace deposits has been identified in the Tas drainage system. The numbering of the terraces relates only to individual drainage basins; however, possible correlations are discussed below.

River terrace deposits have in recent years been regarded largely as cold climate aggradations. It has been argued that the increased precipitation and enhanced slope instability during cold periods led to braided streams with high discharges and an abundant sediment supply. At several localities, organic horizons are associated with the terrace deposits, enabling a provisional chronology to be established.

DETAILS

Waveney–Little Ouse drainage basins

Terraces at four levels can be recognised (Table 7).

The highest terrace (fourth) is preserved only in the lower reaches of the Waveney valley east of Needham [226 815]. The terrace lies 5 to 9 m above the adjacent floodplain at between 20 and 25 m above OD. There is no exposure of the deposits forming this terrace within the district, although they have been dug extensively for aggregate around Shotford Heath [245 815]. Borehole TM28SE/32 [2741 8454] proved 3.0 m of these deposits, which comprise a flint-rich sandy gravel (Auton et al., 1985).

Downstream, beyond the district, this terrace continues as the Homersfield Terrace (Sparks and West, 1968; Coxon, 1979, 1984). Between Homersfield and Flixton, its deposits are exposed in extensive gravel workings. The thickness and stratigraphy of the terrace

Table 7 River terraces in the Waveney–Little Ouse drainage basin.

Local terrace number	Elevation above present-day floodplain		Terrace name
4	5.0–9.0 m		Homersfield Terrace
3	3.0–4.0 m	difficult to separate in some areas	Broome Terrace
2	1.0–3.0 m		
1	0.5–1.0 m		Floodplain Terrace

deposits in these workings are the subjects of some dispute. Coxon (1979, 1984) regarded them as a thick, complex sequence of sands and gravels which also include thin chalky clays which he interpreted as flow tills. He cited the existence of ice-collapse structures and a variable downstream terrace gradient as further evidence for the proximity of ice during aggradation. Based on these observations, a late Anglian fluvioglacial origin was suggested by Coxon (1984). Subsequent investigations (Horton, 1982a; Clarke et al., 1984) suggested, however, that only the upper part of the sequence described by Coxon belongs to the terrace aggradation. These authors believed that the terrace simply comprises up to 4.5 m of flint-rich gravels which rest on Anglian glacial deposits and quartz- and quartzite-rich gravels (Beccles Beds). A late Anglian age for the deposits cannot be excluded, though they are probably younger.

Small patches of third terrace deposits have been mapped in the Little Ouse and Waveney drainage systems west of Oakley. There, the terrace lies between 3 and 4 m above the adjacent floodplain. East of Oakley, the third terrace has not been separately identified and it may merge with the lower, second terrace (Lawson, 1982). Third terrace deposits have been encountered in only one borehole, TM07NE/43 [0965 7929], which proved 6.0 m of pebbly sand that becomes progressively silty towards its base. The clasts are predominantly of angular and subangular flints, with some flint pebbles.

Deposits of the second terrace are exposed extensively along the Little Ouse and Waveney valleys, and locally within their tributaries. The terrace is best preserved in the western part of the Waveney valley and the Little Ouse valley. Boreholes through the deposits show that they are generally 3 to 8 m thick, with a maximum recorded thickness of 8.4 m in TM07NE/40 [0864 7984], west of Roydon. Generally, they comprise gravelly sand or sand with sporadic clasts, mostly angular flints. The base of these deposits commonly lies several metres below the present floodplain.

The second and third terraces probably correspond to the Broome Terrace described farther east, down the Waveney valley (Sparks and West, 1968; Coxon, 1984). At Broome Heath Pit, the Broome Terrace deposits contain sandy and silty lenses with pollen (Coxon, 1984). The type X palynomorph characteristic of the Hoxnian interglacial is present in small quantities as reworked material. Since the terrace level lies at a higher elevation than the nearby Ipswichian deposit at Wortwell, it has been suggested that the deposits are Wolstonian in age (Coxon, 1984).

The first (Floodplain) terrace of the Waveney–Ouse drainage systems forms a low bench between 0.5 and 1.0 m above the present floodplain. Deposits of this terrace have been mapped throughout the lengths of the two rivers and in many of their tributaries. In the western parts of the main Waveney–Little Ouse valley, the deposits are commonly more than 5.0 m thick, with a maximum recorded thickness of 11.1 m in borehole TM08SE/22 [0673 8059], at Fen Street. They are generally less than 4 m thick in the east, although a distinction between the terrace deposits and the underlying glacial sand and gravel may not be obvious (Auton et al., 1985). The deposits are mostly fine- to medium-grained sands with seams of angular flints and quartzite pebbles, which occur especially as a lag deposit at the base of the sequence. At Shotford, the deposits have yielded a cold climate fauna of Coelodonta antiquitatis (woolly rhinoceras) and Mammathus primigenius (woolly mammoth) (Coxon, 1984).

The first terrace deposits become coarser downstream, east of the district; a locality at Wortwell [2752 8437], just beyond the district boundary, shows Ipswichian deposits beneath the first terrace gravels (Sparks and West, 1968; Coxon, 1984). Farther east, a temporary section [327 899] near Earsham revealed peat beneath first terrace deposits; this peat has been radiocarbon dated at 11 210 years BP (Auton et al., 1985) and has yielded a beetle fauna indicating cold climatic conditions (Taylor and Coope, 1985). Other Late Devensian organic remains have been found in hollows resting on the first terrace deposits at Little Fen [042 794] (Tallantire, 1953), and in the Little Ouse valley (Coxon, 1978; Bradshaw et al., 1981). The first terrace deposits must therefore be Late Devensian in age.

Thet drainage basin

Two terraces have been identified in the upper reaches of the River Thet and its tributaries in the north-west of the district.

The second terrace lies between 5 and 6 m above the floodplain. Although not exposed, the overlying soils suggest that the deposits comprise yellowish brown sands and gravels. Angular to subangular flints are the dominant clasts. By comparison with the Waveney valley, the altitude of this terrace suggests that these deposits are either Wolstonian or late Anglian in age.

The first terrace lies up to 3 m above the adjacent alluvium surface and has a similar composition to the second terrace. The deposits are exposed in Minns Pit [003 940], north-west of Shropham, where they extend beneath alluvium. Here they comprise up to 7 m of coarse flint-rich gravels which contain organic silts and clays near the base of the sequence. These first terrace deposits occur higher above the alluvium than the first terrace in the Waveney valley, and are not necessarily of the same age.

Tas drainage basin

A single small patch of sandy gravel [2345 9381], south-west of Hempnall, forms a terrace feature between 1 and 2 m above the floodplain.

Cover sand

On the till-covered plateau to the south of the River Tas valley, between Stratton St Michael and Hempnall, there is a patchy veneer of cover sand which rarely exceeds 1 m in thickness. Because of its impersistence and thinness, the deposit has not been mapped. It was exposed in the south face of Morningthorpe Gravel Pit [2180 9428] where it comprised up to 0.4 m of orange-brown, medium- to coarse-grained, apparently well-sorted sand with a few scattered small flints. Its base was irregularly festooned into the underlying till.

The origin of the deposit is uncertain. Its uniformity and good sorting suggest that it may be wind-blown sand, but the sporadic occurrence of flints and gravelly streaks implies that, at least in part, it has been reworked and water-laid. The age of the cover sand is not known, but it is probably Devensian. Similar deposits occur more extensively in Breckland, on the adjoining Thetford and Bury St Edmunds sheets; their lithology, genesis and age are discussed by Bristow (1990).

Flandrian deposits

Outcrops of Flandrian (Holocene) deposits within the district comprise alluvium, peat, shell marl and calcareous tufa. Excepting the calcareous tufa, the deposits are developed along the valley floors. Flandrian mere deposits are not shown on the published map.

The deposits were laid down after the end of the last (Devensian) glaciation, about 10 000 years ago. Indeed, many of the deposits are considerably younger and, in places, where man has not modified the drainage and landscape, they continue to form today.

Alluvium

Alluvium occurs along the valleys of the Tas, Thet, Little Ouse and Waveney drainage systems. The deposit generally comprises a stiff, greyish brown-mottled, variably sandy and silty clay. It tends to be sandier in constricted parts of the valleys where hillwash contributes more sandy material. It also contains interbeds of humic clay or peat, and can pass laterally into more substantial peat deposits.

These deposits rest on gravels, which may form part of the alluvium or may be co-extensive with the terrace deposits, and also locally on head. Over much of the district, the alluvium thickness averages about 1.0 m, although locally up to 2.2 m have been proved.

Shell marl

A single outcrop [163 781] of shell marl occurs north of Oakley. It comprises a thin, calcareous silty clay with numerous freshwater gastropod shells, resting on peat. This sequence was considered by Horton (1982a) to have accumulated in a small backwater of the River Waveney.

Peat

Peat is a partially decomposed mass of vegetation which accumulates in wet ground conditions such as marshes and bogs, and the fringes of shallow lakes. The deposit is extensively developed along the valleys of the Waveney, Little Ouse, Thet and Tas drainage systems. Within these valleys the peat is generally less than 2.0 m thick and interdigitates with, and passes laterally into alluvium. The peat is commonly sandy, especially in narrower valleys where hillwash has contributed to the deposit. Patches of peat also occur as the youngest deposit of depressions infilled with Flandrian mere deposits.

Locally, the peat contains abundant shell debris, which has been examined from four localities in the south-west of the district (Graham in Bristow, 1986). The fauna present in samples collected from shallow ditch excavations along the Ouse–Waveney valley system is listed in Table 8. The assemblages are typical of slow-moving river and marsh environments and are dominated by the gastropods Bithynia, Lymnaea, Planorbis, Carychium, Trichia and Valvata. Species of the bivalve Pisidium are also common. Peat has tended to accumulate in poorly drained stretches of the rivers which were originally fens or marshes, many of which have been subsequently drained.

Calcareous tufa

A small outcrop of calcareous tufa [104 765] occurs west of Thrandeston. The deposit has been recorded in shallow sections and comprises chalk silt with small chalk clasts and tufaceous clays, resting on till. A thickness of about 1 m was recorded by Horton (1982a).

Mere deposits

Thick sequences of Flandrian mere deposits occur in several parts of the district. The sediments accumulated in depressions, some of which are still occupied totally, or partially, by a lake or mere, whilst others which have been infilled with sediment are now blanketed by peat. In the latter case the depressions can only be located by drilling or excavation.

Flandrian sediments, some 17 m thick, occur at about 7 m beneath the surface of The Mere [116 798] at Diss (Peglar et al., 1984). They comprise 4 m of dark plant detritus-rich mud, overlying 5 m of calcareous mud with fine plant detritus, overlying 3 m of laminated mud with about 1 mm thick couplets of pale and dark hue, resting on 5 m of calcareous fine-detritus mud with silt and clay lenses. The chemical composition and fauna of the rhythmically laminated sediments within the sequence can be related to seasonal changes in the environment. Comparison of the pollen spectra within these laminated sediments with other radiocarbon and pollen-dated Flandrian sequences suggests that they were laid down between about 5.5 and 2.5 thousand years BP. The deposits appear to be confined within the mere which is enclosed by till, glacial sand and gravel and, on the south, by river terrace deposits. There is no evidence of pre-Flandrian sedimentation. The origin of The Mere is uncertain; it may relate to subsidence caused by solution of the Chalk beneath the Drift cover (Peglar et al., 1984).

Dickleburgh Moor lies within a circular hollow enclosed and underlain by till. Peat occurs at the surface and some 2 to 3 m of vertical shrinkage has occurred since the Moor was drained in the 1950s. A borehole, TM18SE/27 [1735 8318], proved 14.3 m of peat, peaty clays and shell marls resting on till (Wilcox and Lawson, 1982). Samples from shallow auger holes [1729 8305 and 1716 8300] yielded an almost entirely aquatic fauna (Table 8) dominated by the freshwater gastropods Valvata piscinalis and Bithynia tentacula (Graham in Wilcox and Lawson, 1982). A small mere [133 802] surrounded by peat occurs in the same tributary valley, southwest of Frenze Hall, near Diss.

A second depression, enclosed by till as at Dickleburgh Moor, occurs at Old Buckenham Fen [050 920]. Shallow exposures show peat and thin layers of shell marl with freshwater molluscs. The sequence is probably several metres thick and has yielded bones of Cervus capreolus (roebuck) (Bennett, 1884a).

Extensive deposits of peat resting on Chalk have been mapped at Kenninghall Fen [041 875], Hay Fen [036 884], The Carr [023 892] and Copinces Fen [048 882], all of which are near Quidenham in the north-west of the district. Recent excavations near the Mere on Kenninghall Fen have shown that at least 5 to 7 m of Flandrian deposits, consisting of peats overlying muds and silts, are present in this depression. All the depressions are thought to have been formed by subsidence caused by solution of the underlying chalk.

Table 8 Recent molluscs from the Ouse–Waveney river system and Dickleburgh Moor.

	Grove House Farm [056 789]	Hinderclay Church [035 773]	Blo' Norton [006 795]	Thelnetham Fen [016 789]	Dickleburgh Moor [1716 8300]
Acroloxus lacustris (Linné)	1		3	2	
Anisus leucostoma (Millet)					7
A. vortex (Linné)	1	2	5	54	
Armiger crista (Linné)	1	1			16
Bathyomphalus contortus (Linné)	2		58		
Bithynia tentaculata (Linné)	45	28	34	44	50
B. sp.					?3
Carychium minimum Müller	9	2		171	
C. tridentatum (Risso)		4			1
Cepaea hortensis (Müller)				1	
C. nemoralis (Linné)	1	1	6	1	
Cochlicopa lubrica (Müller)	5	4	1		
Gyraulus laevis (Alder)					?1
Lymnaea palustris (Müller)	22	7	8	51	
L. peregra (Müller)	6		2	9	13
L. stagnalis (Linné)				2	
L. truncatula (Müller)	7	13	9	35	3
L. sp.					2
Oxychilus helveticus (Blum)		6		1	
Oxyloma pfeifferi (Rossmässler)	2	19	6	26	
Planorbarius corneus (Linné)	6	3	1	35	3
Planorbis carinatus Müller			2		
P. planorbis (Linné)	12	22	16	68	
Segmentina nitida (Müller)	4				
Trichia sp.	4	49	1	1	
Vallonia excentrica Sterki	9	2			
V. pulchella (Müller)			6		1
Valvata cristata Müller	14	10		36	7
V. piscinalis (Müller)			8		837
Vertigo antivertigo (Draparnaud)	5	3	3		
Vitrea?					2
Viviparus contectus (Millet)	2	5	2	4	
V. sp. [juveniles]			5		
Zenobiella subrufescens (Miller)				3	
Anadonta cygnea (Linné)				1	
Pisidium amnicum (Müller)			35	11	
P. henslowanum (Sheppard)			3		
P. nitidum Jenyns	26	4	26	45	
P. obtusale (Lamarck)				1	
P. sp.					1
Sphaerium corneum (Linné)				10	

NINE

Economic geology

HYDROGEOLOGY AND WATER SUPPLY

The district lies partly within the Waveney catchment (Hydrometric Area 34) and partly within the Great Ouse catchment (Hydrometric Area 33). The water resources, both surface and underground, are administered by the National Rivers Authority, Anglian Region.

The Chalk is the major aquifer and underlies the entire district. In the east, Crag deposits directly overlie the Chalk with which they are in hydraulic continuity. There is an extensive cover of drift consisting of till which acts either as an aquiclude or an aquitard, and of sands and gravels, either at the base of the till or interbedded within it, which contain groundwater.

The rainfall over the district averages about 850 mm annually. The mean evapotranspiration is of the order of 470 mm/year. However, the extensive till cover severely limits the infiltration to the Chalk and the Crag to some 60 to 65 mm/year, equivalent to approximately 35 million cubic metres annually over the district. There is also outflow, particularly to the south and east, into the Chalk aquifer outside the district, but apparently little inflow.

Surface water supplies in the district comprise almost wholly river and stream intakes, mainly from the rivers Thet and Waveney. There are no large impoundment reservoirs. The total licensed overground water take is about 1.4 million cubic metres per annum (m^3/a), of which 41 per cent is for spray irrigation and 58 per cent for industrial use. No public supply is taken from overground sources.

Groundwater is taken from the Chalk, the sands and gravels, and the Crag. The licensed take from the Chalk amounts to about 11 million m^3/a of which 80 per cent is for public supply, 10 per cent for spray irrigation and 5 per cent for industrial use. The remainder is used for general agricultural purposes and for domestic requirements. The public supply sources all consist of boreholes located near Quidenham [020 876], Bunwell [140 912], Rushall [198 834], Redgrave Fen [046 792], Diss [113 804] and Syleham [209 783].

Approximately 0.4 million m^3/a are taken from the sands and gravels, and from the Crag, mainly from shallow wells and catchpits. About 80 per cent is used for spray irrigation and 2 per cent for industry; the remainder is almost all used for general agricultural purposes, including livestock requirements, since the quality of the groundwater is often inadequate for domestic purposes.

The earliest reference to regional groundwater resources was made by Whitaker (1906, 1921). A catalogue of wells was prepared during the Second World War (Woodland, 1942), and hydrological surveys were carried out by the Ministry of Housing and Local Government (1960, 1963) for the river catchments. More recently, hydrogeological maps were published by the Institute of Geological Sciences (now the British Geological Survey) on a scale of 1:125 000

for northern and for southern East Anglia (1976, 1981). The groundwater resources for the various subcatchments were summarised in Monkhouse and Richards (1982). Finally, a statistical study of borehole yields was made by Monkhouse (1984).

The **Chalk** underlies the whole district, but is exposed only upon the western side. On the eastern side, the Crag directly overlies the Chalk with which it is in hydraulic continuity. The drift cover is very extensive, with very little bedrock exposed anywhere.

The matrix of the Chalk has only limited permeability, and groundwater yielded to boreholes flows through an extensive system of microfissures. The density of fissuring is very variable, and this is reflected by large variations in borehole performance even over distances as short as a few tens of metres. The density of fissuring decreases with depth, and there is likely to be little significant groundwater flow through the Chalk at depths of more than about 100 m beneath the ground surface.

Recorded transmissivities vary from less than 200 cubic metres per day (m^3/d) to, exceptionally, more than 500 m^3/d. The coefficient of storage is generally in the range 0.001 to 0.008, suggesting that the till may form a rather imperfect aquiclude. Expected well yields are also variable. Over most of the district, where the till exceeds 25 m in thickness, or where Crag overlain by till is present, the mean yield of a borehole of 300 mm diameter penetrating 70 m of saturated chalk would be of the order of 2200 cubic metres per day (m^3/d) for a drawdown of 20 m; there would be approximately a 20 per cent chance that the yield would be less than 1200 m^3/d for a drawdown of 30 m. For a borehole of 150 mm diameter penetrating 40 m of saturated chalk the mean yield would be 400 m^3/d for a drawdown of 10 m; there would be approximately a 20 per cent chance that the yield would be less than 300 m^3/d for a drawdown of 20 m. In the western part of the district where the till is absent or less than 25 m in thickness, the Chalk is more permeable and rather more variable. A borehole of 300 mm diameter penetrating 70 m of saturated chalk would have a mean yield of the order of 3300 m^3/d for a drawdown of 20 m, with about a 20 per cent chance of the yield being less than 1200 m^3/d for a drawdown of 30 m. For a borehole of 150 mm diameter, penetrating 40 m of saturated chalk, the mean yield would be about 650 m^3/d for a drawdown of 10 m, with a 20 per cent chance of the yield being less than 250 m^3/d for a drawdown of 20 m.

When a borehole is constructed into the Chalk, the drilling action forms a slurry of water and ground chalk, which forms a 'cake' on the borehole wall. This slurry also tends to enter the fissures through which water would otherwise flow into the borehole. Left in this state, the yield from the borehole may be much less than the potential, and the drawdowns similarly greater. Consequently, it is normal practice to treat the borehole with concentrated hydrochloric acid, which attacks the slurry more readily than the unbroken chalk; the calcium carbonate of the chalk slurry is broken down into carbon dioxide, which is vented from the borehole as a gas, and calcium chloride, which is highly soluble in water and can be easily pumped to waste. Held in the borehole under pressure, the acid may also penetrate and cleanse the fissures in the vicinity of the borehole. Acid treatment of a newly completed borehole generally increases the yield substantially, and sometimes by 100 per cent or more. While the Chalk will generally stand in a borehole without support, thus requiring only a few metres of lining tube near the ground surface, acid treatment is technically difficult unless the lining is carried down beneath the rest water level.

The form of the potentiometric surface of the Chalk groundwater (Figure 12) shows some interesting features. There appears to be little if any inflow to the district from the Chalk of the surrounding areas; indeed, the flow is either westwards towards the Great Ouse Catchment or eastwards beneath the Waveney valley. Thus the only contribution to the groundwater resources comes from infiltration through the till, a situation that is confirmed by the presence of a groundwater 'mound' (where the potentiometric surface lies at more than 40 m above OD running from the northern edge of the district approximately through Carleton Rode [115 925] to Winfarthing [108 858]. The groundwater contours shown on Figure 12 are for late September 1976, at the end of a notable groundwater drought when the potentiometric surface was at its lowest recorded level.

The quality of groundwater in the Chalk is generally good throughout the district. Two typical analyses are shown in Table 9, the Larling site having a borehole constructed through thin, sandy drift into the Chalk, while the Percehall Manor site has a borehole passing through nearly 30 m of dominantly clayey drift with some sand and gravel into the Chalk beneath. Both waters are of the calcium-bicarbonate type, but beneath the thicker drift, the water is rather more mineralised; there are also measurable concentrations of iron and manganese which were probably taken up by water infiltrating through the drift. Where the Chalk has no drift cover, or a thin cover of sandy drift, the groundwater generally contains some nitrate, and this may locally exceed

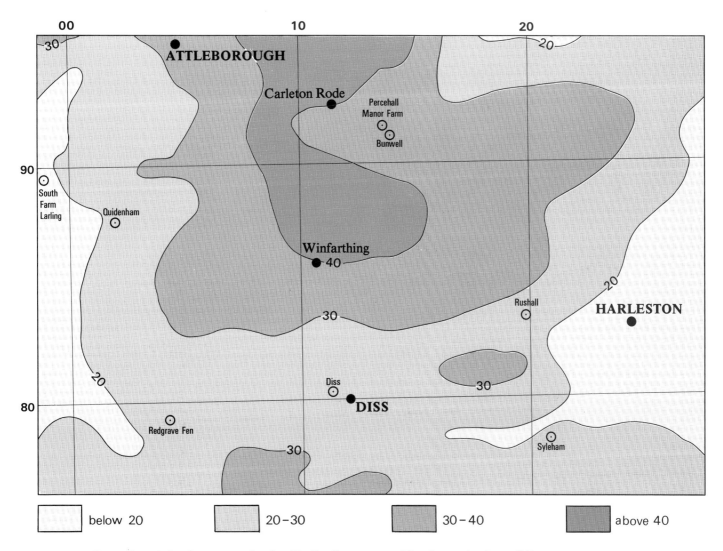

Figure 12 Groundwater-level contours for the Chalk. Contours at 10 m intervals above OD.

Table 9 Typical analyses of groundwater from the Chalk of the district.

Site	South Farm Larling [TL 989 894]	Percehall Manor Farm [137 915]
Analyst	NRA	NRA
Date	16 Oct 1989	11 Jul 1989
pH (pH units)	7.47	7.12
Electrical conductivity (ps/cm)		705
Alkalinity as $CaCO_3$	192	357
Calcium as Ca	99.7	149
Magnesium as Mg	1.82	4.76
Sodium as Na	9.91	13.5
Potassium as K	0.85	1.58
Bicarbonate as HCO_3	234	436
Sulphate as SO_4	26.2	25.3
Chloride as Cl	25.7	26.2
Nitrate as N	3.44	<0.05
Iron as Fe	<0.05	0.03
Manganese as Mn	<0.03	0.07
Fluoride as F		0.24

Units are in milligrammes per litre except where otherwise stated.

NRA = National Rivers Authority.

5 mg/l. Beneath a cover of till, nitrate is rarely present in other than very low concentrations, if present at all.

The **sand and gravel deposits** form a useful if rather small-scale aquifer. The groundwater is generally tapped by shallow shafts and boreholes, and sometimes by catchpits. Yields are usually small, a few hundred cubic metres per day at best. Boreholes are rarely able to stand unsupported, and sand screens and filter packs are required. Shafts are usually supported by open brickwork or 'steining', and occasionally by concrete or metal liners. Where the deposits are exposed at the surface, the groundwater is reasonably soft, with a total hardness of the order of 200 to 300 mg/l, but concentrations of nitrate often exceed 5.0 mg/l and sometimes 10.0 mg/l (as N). Beneath till cover, the total hardness often exceeds 500 mg/l, the greater part being noncarbonate hardness, although the concentration of nitrate is usually negligible. Groundwater from the sands and gravels is frequently ferruginous.

The **Crag** also potentially forms a useful aquifer. However, the presence of fine-grained running sands can make borehole construction difficult. Sand screens and filter packs are essential to prevent borehole collapse. The groundwater quality is very similar to that of the sands and gravels, often being very hard beneath till cover. The proportion of noncarbonate hardness is, however, generally less. The groundwater is almost invariably ferruginous, which militates against its use for domestic purposes. Yields are usually low, of the order of tens to a few hundred cubic metres per day.

The presence of **buried channels** cut into the surface of the Chalk is often an embarrassment to groundwater exploitation. Although the location of many of the major channels has been established, for example that running approximately beneath the present Waveney valley, others may be present but are impossible to predict. Where the infill is clayey, the channel tends to form a barrier to groundwater flow, potentially reducing the yield of adjacent borehole sources. Rather surprisingly, yields from boreholes penetrating the Chalk beneath such channels often yield moderate to good quantities of groundwater, although the cost of such boreholes is much greater due to the additional depth of drilling and the additional lengths of lining tube required. When the infill is predominantly sandy, substantial quantities of groundwater may potentially be drawn from the channel; nevertheless, the sands often have a very fine grain size, are uncemented and tend to run freely. Consequently, the design, emplacement and development of sand screens and filter packs, which are essential to prevent borehole collapse, pose serious problems. The groundwater quality in these deposits is very similar to that in the sands and gravels.

SAND AND GRAVEL

Deposits of sand and gravel are important sources of aggregate for the construction industry. An assessment of them in the southern and eastern part of the district has been completed (Auton, 1982; Wilcox and Stanczyszn, 1983; Auton et al., 1985). At the time of the investigations, four criteria had to be met before the deposit was considered as a potential source of aggregate: i) the average thickness of the deposit had to be at least 1 m; ii) the ratio of overburden to aggregate could not exceed 3:1; iii) the proportion of fine material (<0.063 mm) could not exceed 40 per cent, and iv) the aggregate had to be within 25 m of the surface. On this basis, the detailed analyses of thickness and grain size of mineral, and the thickness of overburden, are given in the above quoted reports. A summary of the results for each resource block is given in Table 10.

The glacial sand and gravel has been dug from several pits; those still operative are at Mount Pleasant [TL 992 951] and on Snetterton Heath [013 900]. The deposits are lithologically very variable and, where clayey, they are used as hoggin. Other recently active, but now partly backfilled pits include those at Roydon [099 802], north-east of Needham [230 823; 226 824] and north of Morningthorpe [218 944].

The major source of aggregate is the river terrace deposits. They have been extensively dug along the flood plain of the River Thet in the north-west, where Minns Pit [003 940] is still operative. Along the Waveney Valley, the river terrace deposits are being dug extensively around Shotford Heath [245 815].

LIMESTONE

The soft limestones of the Chalk have been dug for lime wherever they crop out but there are no workings at the present time. The Lowestoft Till has been dug from numerous pits to marl light sandy soils.

Table 10 Statistical assessment of the sand and gravel resources.

Resource block	Area		Mean thickness		Volume of mineral	Limits at the 95% probability level		Mean grading percentages						
	Block	Mineral	Over-burden	Mineral			± volume	Fines	Sand			Gravel		
	km²	km²	m	m	10⁶m³	± %	10⁶m³	$-\frac{1}{16}$	$+\frac{1}{16}-\frac{1}{4}$	$+\frac{1}{4}-1$	$+1-4$	$+4-16$	$+16-64$	$+64$ mm
DRIFT DEPOSITS ONLY														
TM 07 (98)	150.0	95.3	8.1	6.8	658	14	92	10	33	35	6	9	7	0
TM 17 (121)	146.7	109.9	9.4	10.6	1178	11	130	7	29	43	6	9	6	
TM 27 (?)	144.0	139.7	7.7	9.9	1385	9	125							
CRAG ONLY								Data not processed						
TM07 (28)	—	38.2	11.8	5.6	214	20	43	10	56	30	2	1	1	0
TM17 (56)	—	68.9	—	9.9	682	15	102	7	48	42	2	1	0	

Figures within brackets show the total number of sample points used

BRICK CLAYS

Materials suitable for brickmaking are rare. Clays were dug from the glacial lake deposits around Banham until the 1950s, and the interglacial silt and clay of the Hoxne Beds at Oakley Park [175 767] have been almost totally worked out. The Lowestoft Till has been used in historic times to make unburnt straw bricks, and the weathered material as a plaster on loosely woven hazel laths (wattle and daub) to make walls for timber-framed cottages.

REFERENCES

Most of the references listed below are held in the Library of the British Geological Survey at Keyworth, Nottingham. Copies of the references can be purchased subject to the current copyright legislation.

ALLEN, P. 1984. *Field guide to the Gipping and Waveney valleys, Suffolk. May, 1982.* (Cambridge: Quaternary Research Association.)

AUTON, C A. 1982. The sand and gravel resources of the country around Redgrave, Suffolk. Description of 1:25 000 sheet TM 07 and part of TM 08. *Mineral Assessment Report Institute of Geological Sciences*, No. 117.

— MORIGI, A N, and PRICE, D. 1985. *The sand and gravel resources of the country around Harleston and Bungay, Norfolk and Suffolk. Description of 1:25 000 resource sheets comprising parts of TM27, 28, 38 and 39.* (Keyworth: British Geological Survey.)

BADEN-POWELL, D R W. 1948. The chalky boulder clays of Norfolk and Suffolk. *Geological Magazine*, Vol. 85, 279–296.

— 1950. Field meeting in the Lowestoft district. *Proceedings of the Geologists' Association*, Vol. 61, 191–197.

BANHAM, P. 1971 Pleistocene beds at Corton, Suffolk. *Geological Magazine*, Vol. 108, 281–285.

BECK, R B, FUNNELL, B M, and LORD, A R. 1972. Correlation of the Lower Pleistocene Crag at depth in Suffolk. *Geological Magazine*, Vol. 109, 137–139.

BENNETT, F J. 1884a. The geology of the country around Attleborough, Watton and Wymondham (explanation of Quarter-Sheet 66 SW). *Memoir of the Geological Survey of Great Britain.*

— 1884b. The geology of the country around Diss, Botesdale and Ixworth (explanation of Quarter-Sheet 50 NW). *Memoir of the Geological Survey of Great Britain.*

BLOODWORTH, A J. 1986. Clay mineralogy as an indicator of the provenance of certain East Anglian tills. *Mineralogy and Petrology Report British Geological Survey*, No. 86/12.

BOATMAN, A R C. 1977. Depositional environment of the Red Crag. Unpublished PhD thesis, University of London.

BOSWELL, P G H. 1931. The stratigraphy of the glacial deposits in East Anglia in relation to early man. *Proceedings of the Geologists' Association*, Vol. 42, 87–111.

BRADSHAW, R H W, COXON, P, GREIG, J R A, and HALL, A R. 1981. New fossil evidence for the past cultivation and processing of hemp (*Cannabis sativa L.*) in eastern England. *New Phytologist*, Vol. 89, 503, 510.

BRIDGE, D McC, and HOPSON, P M. 1985. Fine gravel, heavy mineral and grain-size analyses of mid-Pleistocene glacial deposits in the lower Waveney valley, East Anglia. *Modern Geology*, Vol. 9, 129–144.

BRISTOW, C R. 1980. The geology of the country around Walsham le Willows. (Explanation of 1:10 560 geological sheet TM 07 SW). *Open-file Report, Institute of Geological Sciences*, No. 1980/6.

— 1983. The stratigraphy and structure of the Crag of mid-Suffolk, England. *Proceedings of the Geologists' Association*, Vol. 94, 1–12.

— 1986. *Geological notes and local details for 1:10 000 sheets TM 07 NW and NE (Botesdale and Wortham).* (Keyworth: British Geological Survey.)

— 1990. Geology of the country around Bury St Edmunds. *Memoir of the British Geological Survey*, Sheet 189 (England and Wales).

— and COX, F C. 1973. The Gipping Till, a reappraisal of East Anglian glacial stratigraphy. *Quarterly Journal of the Geological Society of London*, Vol. 129, 1–37.

BRITISH GEOLOGICAL SURVEY. 1985. Map 1—Pre-Permian geology of the United Kingdom (South). Map 2—Contours on the top of the Pre-Permian surface of the United Kingdom.

BRYDONE, R M. 1931. The course of *Marsupites* and *Uintacrinus* across Norfolk. *Transactions of the Norfolk and Norwich Naturalists' Society*, Vol. 13, 115–118.

— 1932. *Uintacrinus* in North Suffolk. *Journal of the Ipswich and District Natural History Society*, Vol. 1, Part 3, 158–161.

CASEY, R, and GALLOIS, R W. 1973. The Sandringham Sands of Norfolk. *Proceedings of the Yorkshire Geological Society*, Vol. 40, 1–22.

CLARKE, M R. 1983. The sand and gravel resources of the country around Woolpit, Suffolk. Description of 1:25 000 sheet TL 96. *Mineral Assessment Report Institute of Geological Sciences*, No. 127.

— and AUTON, C A. 1984. Ingham Sand and Gravel. 14 in *Field guide to the Gipping and Waveney valleys, Suffolk. May, 1982.* ALLEN, P (editor). (Cambridge: Quaternary Research Association.)

— WILCOX, C J, and HORTON, A. 1984. The Homersfield Terrace—investigations post-1979. 86–88 in *Field guide to the Gipping and Waveney valleys, Suffolk. May, 1982.* ALLEN, P (editor). (Cambridge: Quaternary Research Association.)

CORNWELL, J D. 1985. Applications of geophysical methods to mapping unconsolidated sediments in East Anglia. *Modern Geology*, Vol. 9, 187–205.

COX, F C. 1981. The 'Gipping Till' revisited. 32–42 in *The Quaternary in Britain*. NEALE, J, and FLENLEY, J (editors). (Oxford: Pergamon.)

— 1985. The tunnel-valleys of Norfolk, East Anglia. *Proceedings of the Geologists' Association*, Vol. 96, 357–369.

— GALLOIS, R W, and WOOD, C J. 1989. Geology of the country around Norwich. *Memoir of the British Geological Survey*, Sheet 161 (England and Wales).

— and NICKLESS, E F P. 1972. Some aspects of the glacial history of central Norfolk. *Bulletin of the Geological Survey of Great Britain*, No. 42, 79–98.

COXON, P. 1978. The first record of a fossil naled in Britain. *Quaternary Newsletter*, No. 24, 9–11.

— 1979. Pleistocene environmental history in central East Anglia. Unpublished PhD thesis, University of Cambridge.

— 1984. The Waveney Valley. 78–107 in *Field guide to the Gipping and Waveney valleys, Suffolk. May, 1982.* ALLEN, P (editor). (Cambridge: Quaternary Research Association.)

DIXON, R G. 1979. Sedimentary facies in the Red Crag (Lower Pleistocene, East Anglia). *Proceedings of the Geologists' Association*, Vol. 90, 117–132.

EHLERS, J, and LINKE, G. 1989. The origin of deep buried channels of Elsterian age in north-west Germany. *Journal of Quaternary Science*, Vol. 4, 255–265.

FRERE, J. 1800. Account of flint weapons discovered at Hoxne in Suffolk. *Archaeologica*, Vol. 18, 204.

FUNNELL, B M, NORTON, P E P, and WEST, R G. 1979. The Crag at Bramerton, near Norwich, Norfolk. *Philosphical Transactions of the Royal Society of London*, Series B, Vol. 287, 489–534.

— and WEST, R G. 1977. Preglacial Pleistocene deposits of East Anglia. 247–265 in *British Quaternary studies: recent advances*. SHOTTON, F W (editor). (Oxford: Oxford University Press.)

GALLOIS, R W, and MORTER, A A. 1982. The stratigraphy of the Gault of East Anglia. *Proceedings of the Geologists' Association*, Vol. 93, 351–368.

GIBBARD, P L, and ZALASIEWICZ, J A (editors). 1988. *Pliocene – Middle Pleistocene of East Anglia. Field guide*. (Cambridge: Quaternary Research Association.)

GLADFELTER, B G. 1975. Middle Pleistocene sedimentary sequences in East Anglia (United Kingdom). 225–258 in *After the Australopithecines*. BUTZER, K W, and ISSAC, G L (editors). (The Hague: Mouton.)

HANCOCK, J M. 1975. The petrology of the Chalk. *Proceedings of the Geologists' Association*, Vol. 86, 499–535.

HARMER, F W. 1900. The Pliocene deposits of East of England: Part II. The Crag of Essex (Waltonian) and its relation to that of Suffolk and Norfolk. *Quarterly Journal of the Geological Society of London*, Vol. 56, 705–744.

— 1902. A sketch of the later Tertiary history of East Anglia. *Proceedings of the Geologists' Association*, Vol. 17, 417–479.

— 1909. The Pleistocene Period in the eastern counties of England. *Proceedings of the Geologists' Association*, Vol. 21, 103–123.

HEWITT, H D. 1924. Notes on some Chalk sections in the district around Thetford, Norfolk. *Proceeding of the Geologists' Association*, Vol. 35, 220–244.

— 1935. Further notes on the Chalk of the Thetford district, Norfolk. *Proceedings of the Geologists' Association*, Vol. 46, 18–37.

HEY, R W. 1967. The Westleton Beds reconsidered. *Proceedings of the Geologists' Association*, Vol. 78, 427–445.

— 1980. Equivalents of the Westland Green Gravels in Essex and East Anglia. *Proceedings of the Geologists' Association*, Vol. 91, 279–290.

—and BRENCHLEY, P J. 1977. Volcanic pebbles from Pleistocene gravels in Norfolk and Essex. *Geological Magazine*, Vol. 114, 219–225.

HOPSON, P M, and BRIDGE, D McC. 1987. Middle Pleistocene stratigraphy in the lower Waveney valley, East Anglia. *Proceedings of the Geologists' Association*, Vol. 98, 171–185.

HORTON, A. 1970. The drift sequence and subglacial topography in parts of the Ouse and Nene Basin. *Report of the Institute of Geological Sciences*, No. 70/9.

— 1982a. *Geological notes and local details for 1:10 000 sheets TM 17 NW, NE, SW and SE (Diss, Hoxne, Eye and Occold)*. (Keyworth: Institute of Geological Sciences.)

— 1982b. *Geological notes and local details for 1:10 000 sheets TM 27 NW, NE and SW (Brockdish, Norfolk, and Stradbroke, Suffolk)*. (Keyworth: Institute of Geological Sciences.)

— 1989. Geology of the Peterborough district. *Memoir of the British Geological Survey*, Sheet 158 (England and Wales).

INSTITUTE OF GEOLOGICAL SCIENCES. 1976. Hydrogeological map of northern East Anglia. Scale 1:125 000.

— 1981. Hydrogeological map of southern East Anglia. Scale 1:125 000.

— 1988. Hydrological data UK: Hydrometric register and statistics 1981–85. (Wallingford: Institute of Hydrology.)

KEMP, R A. 1985. The Valley Farm Soil in southern East Anglia. 179–195 in *Soils and Quaternary landscape evolution*. BOARDMAN, J (editor). (New York: Wiley.)

LAWSON, T E. 1982. *Geological notes and local details for 1:10 000 sheets TM 28 NW, NE, SW and SE (Harleston, Norfolk)*. (Keyworth: Institute of Geological Sciences.)

MATHERS, S J. 1988. *Geological notes and local details for 1:10 000 sheets TM 08 NW, NE 09 SW, SE and parts of TL 98 NE, 99 SE (Kenninghall, Banham, Attleborough and Old Buckenham)*. (Keyworth: British Geological Survey.)

— and ZALASIEWICZ, J A. 1988. The Red Crag and Norwich Crag formations of southern East Anglia. *Proceedings of the Geologists' Association*, Vol. 99, 261–278.

— — BLOODWORTH, A J, and MORTON, A C. 1987. The Banham Beds—a petrologically distinct suite of Anglian glacigenic deposits from central East Anglia. *Proceedings of the Geologists' Association*, Vol. 98, 229–240.

MAYHEW, D F. 1985. Preliminary report of research project on small mammal remains from British Lower Pleistocene sediments. *Quaternary Newsletter*, No. 47, 1–4.

— and STUART, A J. 1986. Stratigraphic and taxonomic revision of the fossil vole remains (Rodentia: microtinae) from the Lower Pleistocene deposits of eastern England. *Philosophical Transactions of the Royal Society of London*, Series B, Vol. 312, 431–485.

MINISTRY OF HOUSING AND LOCAL GOVERNMENT. 1960. Hydrological survey: River Great Ouse Basin, Hydrometric Area No. 33. (London: HMSO.)

— 1963. Hydrological survey: East Anglian rivers, Hydrometric Areas Nos. 34 & 35. (London: HMSO.)

MITCHELL, G F, PENNY, L F, SHOTTON, F W, and WEST, R G. 1973. A correlation of Quaternary deposits in the British Isles. *Special Report of the Geological Society of London*, No. 4.

MONKHOUSE, R A, and RICHARDS, H J. 1982. *Groundwater resources of the United Kingdom*. Commission of the European Communities. (Hannover: Th. Schäfer.)

— 1984. A statistical study of specific capacities of boreholes in the Chalk of East Anglia and their use in predicting borehole yields. *Institute of Geological Sciences, Open-File Report*, WD/84/2.

MORTER, A A, and WOOD, C J. 1983. The biostratigraphy of Upper Albian – Lower Cenomanian *Aucellina* in Europe. *Zitteliana*, Vol. 10, 515–529.

MORTIMORE, R N, and WOOD, C J. 1986. The distribution of flint in the English Chalk, with particular reference to the 'Brandon Flint Series' and the high Turonian flint maximum. In *The scientific study of flint and chert: papers from the Fourth International Flint Symposium*, Vol. 1. SIEVEKING, G, and HART, M B (editors). (Cambridge University Press.)

MURRAY, K H. 1986. Correlation of electrical resistivity marker bands in the Cenomanian and Turonian Chalk from the London Basin to East Yorkshire. *Report of the British Geological Survey*, Vol. 17, No. 8.

PEAKE, N B, and HANCOCK, J M. 1961. The Upper Cretaceous of Norfolk. *Transactions of the Norfolk and Norwich Naturalists' Society*, Vol 19, 293–339.

PEGLAR, S M, FRITZ, S C, ALAPIETI, T, SAARNISTO, M, and BIRKS, J B. 1984. Composition and formation of laminated sediments in Diss Mere, Norfolk, England. *Boreas*, Vol. 13, 13–28.

PERRIN, R M S, DAVIES, H, and FYSK, M D. 1973. The lithology of the chalky boulder clay. *Nature, London*, Vol. 245, 101–104.

— ROSE, J, and DAVIES, H. 1979. The distribution, variation and origins of Pre-Devensian tills in Eastern England. *Philosophical Transactions of the Royal Society of London*, Series B, Vol. 287, 536–569.

ROSE, J, and ALLEN, P. 1977. Middle Pleistocene stratigraphy in south-east Suffolk. *Journal of the Geological Society of London*, Vol. 133, 85–102.

— ALLEN, P, and HEY, R W. 1976. Middle Pleistocene stratigraphy in southern East Anglia. *Nature, London*, Vol. 263, 492–494.

SHOTTON, F W, and WEST, R G. 1969. Stratigraphical table of the British Quaternary. *Proceedings of the Geological Society of London*, No. 1656, 155–157.

SKERTCHLEY, S B J. 1879. On the manufacture of gun flints. *Memoir of the Geological Survey of Great Britain*.

SPARKS, B W, and WEST, R G. 1968. Interglacial deposits at Wortwell, Norfolk. *Geological Magazine, Vol. 105, 471–481.*

STRAW, A. 1979. The geomorphological significance of the Wolstonian Glaciation of Eastern England. *Transactions of the Institute of British Geographers*, Vol. 4, 540–549.

TALLANTIRE, P A. 1953. Studies in the Post-Glacial history of the British vegetation. XIII, Lopham Little Fen, a Late-Glacial site in central East Anglia. *Journal of Ecology*, Vol. 41, 361–373.

TAYLOR, B J, and COOPE, R G. 1985. Arthropods in the Quaternary of East Anglia—their role as indices of local palaeoenvironments and regional palaeoclimates. *Modern Geology*, Vol. 9, 159–185.

TURNER, C. 1970. The Middle Pleistocene deposits at Marks Tey, Essex. *Philosophical Transactions of the Royal Society of London*, Series B, Vol. 257, 373–440.

WARD, W H, BURLAND, J B, and GALLOIS, R W. 1968. Geotechnical assessment of a site at Mundford, Norfolk, for a large proton accelerator. *Geotechnique*, Vol. 18, 399–431.

WEST, R G. 1956. The Quaternary deposits at Hoxne, Suffolk. *Philosophical Transactions of the Royal Society of London*, Series B. Vol. 239, 265–356.

— and DONNER, J J. 1956. The glaciations of East Anglia and the East Midlands: a differentiation based on stone orientation measurements of the tills. *Quarterly Journal of the Geological Society of London*, Vol. 112, 69–91.

— and NORTON, P E P. 1974. The Icenian Crag of south-east Suffolk. *Philosophical Transactions of the Royal Society of London*, Series B, Vol. 269, 1–28.

WHITAKER, W. 1906. The water supply of Suffolk from underground sources. *Memoir of the Geological Survey* (England and Wales).

— 1921. The water supply of Norfolk from underground sources. *Memoir of the Geological Survey* (England and Wales).

— and DALTON, W H. 1887. The geology of the country around Halesworth and Harleston (explanation of Quarter-Sheet 50 NE). *Memoir of the Geological Survey of Great Britain*.

WILCOX, C J, and LAWSON, T E. 1982. *Geological notes and local details for 1:10 000 sheets TM 18 SW and SE (Diss, Burston and Dickleburgh).* (Keyworth: Institute of Geological Science.)

— and STANCZYSZYN, R. 1983. The sand and gravel resources of the country around Diss, Norfolk. Description of 1:25 000 sheet TM 17 and part of TM 18. *Mineral Assessment Report Institute of Geological Sciences*, No. 137.

WOOD, S W. 1880. The newer Pliocene period of England. *Quarterly Journal of the Geological Society of London*, Vol. 36, 457–528.

WOODLAND, A W. 1942. Water supply from underground sources of Cambridge–Ipswich district, Part IV: Well catalogues for New Series One-Inch Sheets 175 (Diss) and 176 (Lowestoft). *Wartime Pamphlet of the Geological Survey of Great Britain (England and Wales)*, No. 20. 55 pp.

— 1970. The buried tunnel valleys of East Anglia. *Proceedings of the Yorkshire Geological Society*, Vol. 37, 521–578.

WOODWARD, H B. 1881. The geology of the country around Norwich (explanation of Quarter Sheets 66 NE and SE). *Memoir of the Geological Survey of Great Britain*.

WORSSAM, B C, and TAYLOR, J H. 1969. Geology of the country around Cambridge. *Memoir of the British Geological Survey*, Sheet 188 (England and Wales).

WYATT, R J. 1981. *Geological notes and local details for 1:10 000 sheets TM 29 SW and SE (Hempnall and Woodton).* (Keyworth: Institute of Geological Sciences.)

WYMER, J. 1974. Clactonian and Acheulian industries in Britain: their chronology and significance. *Proceedings of the Geologists' Association*, Vol. 130, 391–421.

— 1983. The Lower Palaeolithic site at Hoxne. *Proceedings of the Suffolk Institute of Archaeology and History*, Vol. 35, 169–189.

ZALASIEWICZ, J A. 1988. *Geological notes and local details for 1:10 000 sheets TM 18 NW, NE, 19 SW and SE (Gissing, Pulham Market, Bunwell Street and Long Stratton).* (Keyworth: British Geological Survey.)

— and MATHERS, S J. 1985. Lithostratigraphy of the Red and Norwich Crags of the Aldeburgh–Orford area, south-east Suffolk. *Geological Magazine*, Vol. 122, 287–296.

APPENDIX 1

Abstract of selected borehole logs

Boreholes are identified by their registered numbers in the Survey's 1:10 000 sheet registration system.

Gypsy Lane, Thelnetham (TM07NW/31) [0033 7846]

Drilled in 1980
Surface level +32.9 m

	Thickness m	Depth m
Made ground	0.4	0.4
Lowestoft Till	22.3	22.7
Upper Chalk	1.3	24.0

North-west of Grove House, Redgrave (TM07NE/23) [0542 7959]

Drill in 1980
Surface level +22.5 m

	Thickness m	Depth m
Soil	0.2	0.2
Peat	1.5	1.7
River terrace deposits		
Pebbly sand	3.0	4.7
Glacial sand and gravel (?north-western provenance)	4.2	8.9
Glacial silt and clay	17.1 +	25.0

The Warren, Botesdale (TM07NE/26) [0574 7638]

Drilled in 1980
Surface level +45.1 m

	Thickness m	Depth m
Soil	0.3	0.3
Kesgrave Sands and Gravels		
Very clayey, pebbly sand	2.0	2.3
Silty sand and clay	2.1	4.4
Clayey, pebbly sand	4.0	8.4
Silty sand and clay	1.0	9.4
Sandy gravel	3.1	12.5
Upper Chalk	2.0	14.5

Ling Farm, Wortham (TM07NE/40) [0864 7984]

Drilled in 1980
Surface level +26.1 m

	Thickness m	Depth m
Soil	0.1	0.1
River terrace deposits		
Sand	8.5	8.5
Glacial sand and gravel	0.5	9.0
Glacial silt and clay		
Soft silt	8.0	17.0
Glacial sand and gravel (north-western provenance)		
Very clayey, pebbly sand	0.4	17.4
Upper Chalk	2.0 +	19.4

Pollard Tree Farm, Wortham (TM07NE/43) [0965 7929]

Drilled in 1980
Surface level +25.4 m

	Thickness m	Depth m
Soil	0.3	0.3
River terrace deposits		
Clayey, pebbly sand	6.0	6.3
Glacial sand and gravel (north-western provenance)		
Sandy gravel	6.0	12.3
Gravel	6.2	18.5
Upper Chalk	1.0	19.5

Langfen Farm, South Lopham (TM08SE/18) [0583 8049]

Drilled in 1980
Surface level +27.1 m

	Thickness m	Depth m
Soil	0.4	0.4
River terrace deposits		
Clayey, pebbly sand	3.0	3.4
Glacial silt and clay	16.6	20.0

Bressingham Fen, Bressingham (TM08SE/22) [0673 8059]

Drilled in 1980
Surface level +23.2 m

	Thickness m	Depth m
Soil	0.3	0.3
River terrace deposits		
Clayey sand, pebbly at base	11.1	11.4
Glacial sand and gravel (?north-western provenance)		
Sandy gravel	1.4	12.8
Glacial silt and clay		
Soft silt, mainly	7.2 +	20.0

Fen Lane, Roydon (TM08SE/29) [0917 8038]

Drilled in 1980
Surface level +35.4 m

	Thickness m	Depth m
Soil	0.3	0.3
Cover sand		
Very clayey, pebbly sand	0.3	0.6
Lowestoft Till	3.6	4.2
Glacial silt and clay		
Silt, partly pebbly	3.6	7.8
Lowestoft Till	1.9	9.7
Glacial sand and gravel (north-western provenance)		
Clayey, pebbly sand	3.2	12.9
Lowestoft Till	0.9	13.8

Heath Farm, Snetterton (TM09SW/16) [0010 9229]

Drilled in 1948
Surface level + 25.6 m

	Thickness m	Depth m
Lowestoft Till	52.43	52.43
Glacial sand and gravel (?north-western provenance)		
Sand and chalk	22.55	72.98
Upper Chalk	14.94	89.92

Gaymers Cyder Works, Attleborough (TM09SE/12) [0514 9493]

Drilled in 1929
Surface level + 37.18 m

	Thickness m	Depth m
Lowestoft Till		
Clay	3.05	3.05
Glacial sand and gravel (north-western provenance)		
Sand and gravel	4.87	7.92
Lowstoft Till	33.53	41.45
Glacial sand and gravel (? north-western provenance)		
Sand and chalk cobbles	21.95	63.40
Upper Chalk	28.04 +	91.44

West of New Buckenham Church (TM09SE/18) [0836 9100]

Drilled in 1983
Surface level unrecorded

	Thickness m	Depth m
Soil	0.5	0.5
Lowestoft Till	18.5	19.0
Norwich Crag		
Green sand with pebbles	1.0	20.0
Upper Chalk	150.5	170.5

Toll Gate Farm, Scole (TM18SE/43) [1608 8061]

Date of drilling unrecorded
Surface level unrecorded

	Thickness m	Depth m
Soil	0.3	0.3
Lowestoft Till	12.1	12.4
Glacial sand and gravel (north-western provenance)		
Pebbly sand and sandy gravel	2.6	15.0
Glacial silt and clay		
Silt	1.3	16.3
Lowestoft Till	1.7	18.0
?Kesgrave Sands and Gravels		
Silty, sandy gravel	1.2	19.2
Sand and silt	1.4	20.6
Ingham Sand and Gravel		
Silty, clayey gravel	2.4	23.0
Pebbly, clayey silt	1.0	24.0
Upper Chalk	5.0	29.0

North of Oak Pollard, Wingfield (TM27NW/18) [2209 7852]

Drilled in 1983
Surface level + 42.4 m

	Thickness m	Depth m
Soil	0.4	0.4
Lowestoft Till	6.9	7.3
Chalk raft	0.3	7.6
Glacial sand and gravel (Beccles 'Glacial' Beds)		
Pebbly sand and silt	1.1	18.9
Sand, partly pebbly	6.1	25.0

College Farm, Wingfield (TM27NW/22) [2318 7663]

Drilled in 1983
Surface level + 33.0

	Thickness m	Depth m
Soil	0.3	0.3
Alluvium		
Sandy silt	1.4	1.7
Glacial sand and gravel (Mendham Beds)		
Sand with pebbles	9.3	11.0
Norwich Crag		
Sand	14.0	25.0

Galloping Hall, Wingfield (TM27NW/23) [2383 7592]

Drilled in 1983
Surface level + 50.3 m

	Thickness m	Depth m
Soil	0.2	0.2
Lowestoft Till	15.8	16.0
Starston Till	1.4	17.4
Kesgrave Sands and Gravels		
Palaeosol	2.2	19.6
Pebbly sand on sandy gravel	5.9	25.5

Vales Hall, Fressingfield (TM27NE/6) [2577 7870]

Drilled in 1982
Surface level + 48.4 m

	Thickness m	Depth m
Soil	0.2	0.2
Lowestoft Till	7.5	7.7
Glacial silt and clay		
Silt	0.3	8.0
Lowestoft Till	4.7	12.7
Starston Till	3.6	16.3
Kesgrave Sands and Gravels		
Palaeosol	1.4	17.7
Clayey, pebbly sand	3.3	21.0
?Palaeosol	0.4	21.4
?Westleton Beds		
Sandy gravel	3.6	25.0

Hospital Farm, Alburgh (TM28NE/25) [2538 8918]

Drilled in 1983
Surface level +44.0 m

	Thickness m	Depth m
Made ground	0.5	0.5
Lowestoft Till	18.5	19.0
Starston Till	7.7	26.7
Glacial sand and gravel (Beccles 'Glacial' Beds)		
Gravel	0.2	26.9
Organic (?interglacial) sediments		
Silt	1.2	28.1
Peat	1.1	29.2
Clayey, sandy silt	3.8	33.0
Norwich Crag		
Sand, pebbly towards base	1.5	34.5
Upper Chalk	2.0 +	36.5

Ingram's Lane, Brockdish (TM28SW/39) [2026 8095]

Drilled in 1982
Surface level +47.6 m

	Thickness m	Depth m
Soil	0.2	0.2
Lowestoft Till (?channel fill deposits)		
Silty, sandy clay	11.8	12.0
Clayey sand on sandy gravel	1.9	13.9
Starston Till	1.8	15.7
Ingham Sand and Gravel		
Clayey, sandy gravel	7.3	23.0
?Kesgrave Sands and Gravels		
Pebbly sand, clayey near base	1.5	24.5
Norwich Crag		
Sand, clayey near top	2.5 +	27.0

Mill Hill, Wortwell (TM28SE/32) [2741 8454]

Drilled in 1982
Surface level +20.7 m

	Thickness m	Depth m
Soil	0.4	0.4
River terrace deposits		
Sandy gravel	3.0	3.4
Glacial sand and gravel (channel fill deposits)		
Sandy gravel and pebbly sand	8.1	11.5
Reworked 'Kesgrave-type sands and gravels'		
Pebbly sand	4.3	15.8
Norwich Crag		
Clayey sand	2.0	17.8
Sandy and clayey silt	3.2 +	21.0

44

APPENDIX 2

Geological Survey photographs

Copies of these photographs are deposited for reference in the libraries of the Geological Museum, South Kensington, London SW7 2DE, and of the British Geological Survey, Keyworth NG12 5GG. Black and white, and colour prints and slides can be supplied. All numbers belong to Series A. Numbers 11432–11435 taken by J M Pulsford and the remainder by H J Evans.

11432 Hoxne, Suffolk [175 767]. Hoxnian interglacial deposits (interglacial silt and clay)

11433 Hoxne, Suffolk [175 767]. Head gravel deposit

11434 Hoxne, Suffolk [175 767]. Hoxnian interglacial deposits (interglacial silt and clay)

11435 Hoxne, Suffolk [175 767]. Contact of the Hoxnian interglacial deposits with the chalky boulder clay

13720 Shell and auger drilling near Redgrave, Suffolk [021 775]

13721 Shell and auger drilling near Redgrave, Suffolk [021 775]

13982 Road cutting north of Wortwell [2738 8542]. Water-laid till (Starston Till) with outwash sands (Mendham Beds)

13985 Disused gravel pit, Roydon [099 801]. Tectonised margin between chalky boulder clay (Lowestoft Till) and glacial sand and gravel

13986 Disused gravel pit, Roydon [099 801]. Glacial sand and gravel

13987 Disused gravel pit, Roydon [099 801]. Glacial sand and gravel

13988 Disused gravel pit near Harleston [259 225]. Section in head

13989 General view of Mendham Marshes [267 820]

13990 Disused gravel pit, Mendham [2715 8242]. Type section of Mendham Beds (glacial sand and gravel associated with Starston Till)

13991 The Kennels Pit [1709 7766]. Glacial sand and gravel

13992 The Kennels Pit [1709 7766]. Cryoturbated glacial sand and gravel

13993 Disused gravel pit, Redenhall [2635 8473]. Glacial sand and gravel overlying Mendham Beds (glacial sand and gravel associated with Starston Till)

13994 Sand and gravel pit at Starston [243 844]. Sand and gravel overlying Mendham Beds (glacial sand and gravel associated with Starston Till)

13995 Hot Dog Pit [1720 7888]. Partially cryoturbated glacial sand and gravel

13999 Roydon, near Diss [1002 8005]. Cryoturbated glacial sand and gravel

15066 The Mere, Diss [116 789]. View from the south

APPENDIX 3

BGS open-file reports relating to this district

BRISTOW, C R. 1986. *Geological notes and local details for 1:10 000 sheets TM 07 NW and NE (Botesdale and Wortham).* (Keyworth: British Geological Survey.)

HORTON, A. 1982. *Geological notes and local details for 1:10 000 sheets TM 17 NW, NE, SW and SE (Diss, Hoxne, Eye and Occold).* Keyworth: Institute of Geological Sciences.)

— 1982. *Geological notes and local details for 1:10 000 sheets TM 27 NW, NE and SW (Brockdish, Norfolk and Stradbroke, Suffolk).* Keyworth: Institute of Geological Sciences.)

LAWSON, T E. 1982. *Geological notes and local details for 1:10 000 sheets TM 28 NW, NE, SW and SE (Harleston, Norfolk).* (Keyworth: Institute of Geological Sciences.)

MATHERS, S J. 1988. *Geological notes and local details for 1:10 000 sheets TM 98 NW, NE, 09 SW, SE and parts of TL 98 NE, 99 SE (Kenninghall, Banham, Attleborough and Old Buckenham).* (Keyworth: British Geological Survey.)

WILCOX, C J. 1981. *Geological notes and local details for 1:10 000 sheets TM 08 SW and SE (Garboldisham, Bressingham and Roydon).* (Keyworth: Institute of Geological Sciences.)

— and LAWSON, T E. 1982. *Geological notes and local details for 1:10 000 sheets TM 18 SW and SE (Diss, Burston and Dickleburgh).* (Keyworth: Institute of Geological Sciences.)

WYATT, R J. 1981. *Geological notes and local details for 1:10 000 sheets TM 29 SW and SE (Hempnall and Woodton).* (Keyworth: Institute of Geological Sciences.)

FOSSIL INDEX

Page numbers in italics refer to figures.
Page numbers in bold refer to tables.

GENERAL INDEX

BRITISH GEOLOGICAL SURVEY

Keyworth, Nottingham NG12 5GG
(0602) 363100

Murchison House, West Mains Road, Edinburgh
EH9 3LA 031-667 1000

London Information Office, Natural History Museum
Earth Galleries, Exhibition Road, London SW7 2DE
071-589 4090

The full range of Survey publications is available through the
Sales Desks at Keyworth and at Murchison House, Edinburgh,
and in the BGS London Information Office in the Natural
History Museum Earth Galleries. The adjacent bookshop
stocks the more popular books for sale over the counter. Most
BGS books and reports are listed in HMSO's Sectional List 45,
and can be bought from HMSO and through HMSO agents
and retailers. Maps are listed in the BGS Map Catalogue, and
can be bought BGS approved stockists and agents as well as
direct from BGS.

*The British Geological Survey carries out the geological survey of Great
Britain and Northern Ireland (the latter as an agency service for the
government of Northern Ireland), and of the surrounding continental
shelf, as well as its basic research projects. It also undertakes
programmes of British technical aid in geology in developing countries
as arranged by the Overseas Development Administration.*

*The British Geological Survey is a component body of the Natural
Environment Research Council.*

HMSO publications are available from:

HMSO Publications Centre
(Mail, fax and telephone orders only)
PO Box 276, London SW8 5DT
Telephone orders 071-873 9090
General enquiries 071-873 0011
Queueing system in operation for both numbers
Fax orders 071-873 8200

HMSO Bookshops
49 High Holborn, London WC1V 6HB
(counter service only)
071-873 0011   Fax 071-873 8200
258 Broad Street, Birmingham B1 2HE
021-643 3740   Fax 021-643 6510
33 Wine Street, Bristol BS1 2BQ
0272-264306   Fax 0272-294515
9 Princess Street, Manchester M60 8AS
061-834 7201   Fax 061-833 0634
16 Arthur Street, Belfast BT1 4GD
0232-238451   Fax 0232-235401
71 Lothian Road, Edinburgh EH3 9AZ
031-228 4181   Fax 031-229 2734

HMSO's Accredited Agents
(see Yellow Pages)

And through good booksellers